CU00918579

So you wai ＿＿＿ ᴐr?

A practical guide for students by a student.

By

Pádraic J. Dunne

Acknowledgements

I would like to start by acknowledging Jean Notaro who has been a mentor and a friend to me from the very first evening of my foundation year in counselling and psychotherapy. I am grateful for her advice and contribution toward the theoretical aspects of this book.

I wish to extend my sincere thanks to my classmates and peers with whom I have shared a great deal over the past four years. Their support and friendship has been invaluable throughout. I am particularly grateful to Mary for her contribution to this book.

Special thanks to my father who helped start me on my journey in more ways than one and to my mother who inspired me to become a counsellor in the first place. I miss her every day.

My final thanks goes to J and S; my rock and my scaffold. They are the warm pillow I rest my weary head upon when I feel tired and beat up. They make me smile when I don't feel like smiling.

Table of Contents

Chapter Three Humanistic Schools of Psychotherapy

Chapter Four - Cognitive Behavioural Therapies

Section Two: Studying Counselling

Chapter Five Personal Development

Chapter Ten

Epilogue

Figures

Tables

Chapter One
Introduction

First, don't believe everything you read (or hear) including everything in this book. Take a step back and ask yourself "Is that really true?" You may have no way of verifying the truth of most statements but by thinking about it first, you will have already started to assimilate it into your learning. No teacher, no matter how charismatic and effective can really teach you anything. He or she can only shine a light on an area that has been designed to aid in your personal and professional development. Ultimately, it's up to you to learn and understand it for yourself.

Second, I am an expert in nothing except being a student of counselling and psychotherapy. I will not stand upon a soap box promoting one theoretical school of counselling over another. I will not recount countless tales of my vast clinical experience. The truth is that I am a baby counsellor, still very wet behind the ears. I can only share my experiences as a student of counselling and psychotherapy and some of the experiences of my peers.

Who is this book for?

Do work colleagues confide in you? Do your friends turn to you when their relationships break up or are in trouble? Do people gravitate toward you at the end of parties to offload their worries and fears? If so, the chances are you are a counsellor in waiting and this book is for you.

Are you studying counselling part time and finding it difficult to juggle a day job and/or a family, whilst having a non-existent social life? Have you started clinical placement and are finding it difficult not being able to talk to somebody about your work, apart from your supervisor? If so, you need the support of your peers, who know exactly how you feel. This book is also for you.

The Layout

This book is divided into two sections for your convenience. In the first section you will find a brief summary of the most important schools of counselling and psychotherapy. When I first researched counselling as a potential career I found very little adequate information out there. I knew a little about Sigmund Freud but not much beyond the standard stereotype. I was vaguely aware that Freud developed psychoanalysis but as to other modes of therapy, I remained in the dark. I found a lot of books in my local bookshops in the psychology section but few had anything to do with counselling. The majority were of the self-help variety, while the rest were academic pieces on unfamiliar topics such as humanistic counselling, cognitive behavioural therapy, gestalt psychotherapy, analytical psychology and mindfulness. I didn't know where to start and felt overwhelmed. As a result, I have tried to give you the reader a very basic outline of the major schools. These descriptions are by no means exhaustive and are limited by my inexperience but I hope they can help convey the basic message of what can be complex systems of therapy.

The second section was written with the student of counselling and psychotherapy in mind. In it I will share my experiences of being a student and deal with a variety of subjects, from personal development and assignments to clinical placement and self-care. My experiences are limited to that of a student of counselling in one particular college in Ireland, but I believe that the basic training is similar across most countries. Certainly the trials and tribulations of all of us who study counselling are the same, regardless of where and how you study it.

How to use this book

You don't need to read this book from cover to cover. You might simply want a quick description of what counselling is and the type of schools out there, in which case section one is good enough for you. Of course you might continue on to section two in order to get a sneak preview as to what studying counselling is all about. If you are studying counselling and are feeling anxious about starting your clinical placement, for example, then you can go directly to that section. I have tried to layout the book so that each chapter stands alone; with clear objectives at the start and a summary in point format at the end, followed by some suggested reading where appropriate. I hope you find this book useful. I hope it answers some of your questions and inspires you to study what I believe is a fascinating and noble profession.

My Story

Ever since my teenage years I have wanted to engage in a career in which I could help people. I was always intrigued by biology and so the idea of medicine in some form or another excited me. I ended up studying biomedical science and from there went on to gain a masters in science from the Dublin Institute of Technology as well as a Ph.D. from University College London. The scene was set for an exciting career in medical research as an immunologist. I loved it. I loved supervising student projects, from BSc to MSc to PhD. I loved lecturing and gained experience as much as I could. Not many people realise this but the best researchers are as much artists as they are pragmatists. Creativity plays a huge role in science and I loved that aspect. It is a difficult, frustrating profession with very little remuneration compared with clinical colleagues but the payoff included a flexible work life, filled with creativity and potential. The 95% of sweat always seemed to be worth the 5% of inspiration that might lead to the discovery of something new. To be the first person ever to discover a small but significant component of the immune system was simply exhilarating. I expected a long life in academia, packed with research, teaching and writing. All I needed was a tweed jacket complete with leather elbow patches. Then things started to change.

A slow burning and deep set anger began to envelope me and affect my relationships. I was drinking too much, often alone. I lacked interest in life, which seemed futile and bereft of any sort of justice. I went from someone who had a sense of meaning and purpose to a person hell bent on self-destruction in a nihilistic stupor. To make matters worse my physical health began to decline simultaneously.

In my teens I was diagnosed with Ankylosing Spondylitis, which is a progressive autoimmune disease that targets all joints but particularly those of the spine. Pain from this condition reached its peak in my early twenties and while the medication controlled the progression of the disease, the pain was persistent and affected me day and night; it continues to affect me daily. Stress only exacerbates this pain which is why periods of depression are always associated with enhanced physical pain and distress. In addition to the anger and depression I began to feel very sorry for myself.

Eventually, my partner convinced me to visit a counsellor. At the time I could not see how telling someone about by current predicament could possibly help me. The very idea of it seemed absurd but I went along anyway. It was excruciating at first; the lengthy and embarrassing silences were tortuous. My counsellor seemed nice but offered me no advice, no solutions. She just sat there smiling in what I assumed was the standard counsellor stance. I began to speak, just to break the awful silence and that's when the flood gates opened. I talked and talked for a number of sessions. I felt listed to and understood. I began to see the first outlines of distant memories in my foggy mind. With the help of my counsellor who occasionally coaxed but never coached me, I was able to begin to understand the early origins of my anger. A constant refrain every student of counselling hears is "loss and hurt always lie beneath anger" and this was certainly true for me.

However, just as I was beginning to open doors that were closed since childhood, my brother died suddenly from septicaemia while undergoing a simple appendectomy. Counselling was an enormous help during this difficult time, which was my first real experience of death and all its sudden ferocity. Six months later I left therapy with my counsellor's blessing, still grieving but feeling better about my role and purpose in life. My identity didn't seem so tied to my career as it had previously and so I continued in research.

Soon after, my beautiful daughter was born and we decided to return to Ireland as a family. My partner and I were lucky enough to find two jobs in Trinity College Dublin and a small house in the countryside. The move back was difficult for me; I found it hard to adjust to being close to my family of origin once more after being absent for so long. I found that friends I had before leaving for London had moved on in their lives without me. Of course they had everyday right to but I found this very difficult. My job in Trinity College wasn't all it was cracked up to be either. The true nature of the vicious politics that permeates academia reared its head for the first time. The lack of compassion and respect for employees was difficult to bear at times and so I began to sink back into familiar patterns of anger, supported by drinking and the inevitable decline in physical health.

Everything I had learned in counselling had disappeared and in an attempt to rescue myself I started to read everything I could, from self-help books to existential philosophy to in-depth descriptions of the various world religions. I was searching for meaning, for purpose yet again. As I read, I began to find common threads in many books about the secrets to calming the mind and finding peace.

It seemed that many of these sages recommended a refocusing of attention from oneself onto the needs of others, as a solution to personal depression and anxiety. Acceptance and forgiveness were also prescribed as key tenets of happiness. To forgive others and oneself is easier said than done, at least for me but I recognised it as an essential path to balance in any life. I now consider acceptance as one of the cornerstones of therapy in any guise. By accepting yourself and your position in the world you become more tolerant of emotional and physical pain as well as the perceived slights issued by those around you. It is of course easy for me to write about acceptance and much harder to accomplish it in the real world. For me, daily meditation is the key to greater acceptance and forgiveness. To not engage in medication daily is to allow the tide of doubt, fear and anger to creep over me, as I'm sure my family will attest to. With greater self-awareness often comes greater pain, at least temporarily, as you are exposed to long since hidden shadows. Practicing meditation, acceptance and forgiveness continues to help me to create space between my constant cycling negative thoughts and my emotional responses. Of course it doesn't always work; sometimes I find it hard to accept and forgive.

Around this time I reluctantly came to the conclusion that a career as a scientist in medical research no longer made me happy. My career had stood still and the thought of another 35 years of mediocrity, playing politics and suffering daily stress, filled me with dread. Research it seemed had also rejected me; I did not have the constitution to proceed. It took time to come to terms with the embarrassment of having failed in my chosen career; I had sacrificed a great deal of my life in the name of academia and research. I dreaded the prospect of telling family and friends.

One Saturday afternoon, I sat down with my long suffering partner and we mulled over alternative career choices. I really didn't have a clue. I considered the aspects of research that made me happy: teaching, mentoring others and the intent to make some contribution toward the greater good. In short, I enjoyed helping others feel better and so I started from that basis. Ironically, this was the position from which I entered biomedical research in the first place. I considered a number of options, talked to a number of people in these different areas and provisionally settled with counselling.

Around this time my mother was diagnosed with an aggressive brain tumour. My family and I were helpless observers as she physically disintegrated before our eyes. Needless to say, this was devastating for all of us, not least my mother. The actions of medical staff confounded the unfolding trauma. I was struck again and again by their cold and apathetic responses, with very few exceptions. I remember being brought to tears when a member of the hospital catering staff offered me a cup of tea at 4:30 am, as I sat beside my dying mother. I think it was the isolation of this beautiful act of kindness that affected me so much. That woman's gentle words and kind face meant more to me than she will ever know. Amidst my sadness, helplessness and anger about the situation I began to think that no family should ever be left like this, surrounded by desensitised medical professionals without anyone to speak with. I realised the power of a kind word and this finalised my decision to become a counsellor. My mother was released from her torture three days later. I started a foundation course in counselling and psychotherapy three months after she died and have not regretted my decision since.

I should point out that I did not experience any of the difficulties life offered me thus far alone. I have always been fortunate to have supporting and loving family members and friends. In later years I have been blessed with a loving partner and daughter. However, sometimes the love of close ones is not enough to prevent a descent into sadness and that's where counselling can help. In the past I have asked "Why would anyone need to see a counsellor if they have family and friends?" It is a question I have been asked many times since; it's a fair question. Ask yourself, how many people do you know who truly listen to you, without waiting for their turn to speak and without their own agenda, no matter how loving? Everybody has their blind spot regarding themselves and others. If your blind spot overlaps with that of a family member or friend then you will not really address your issue because you won't be able to see it. We all have personal agendas. It might be the loving agenda of a mother who is blinded by her need to keep her adult child safe but fails to see what this child actually needs.

A good counsellor should not have any hidden agenda. He or she is not emotionally tied to you and therefore won't react unexpectedly or out of turn. A good counsellor will neither push you into acting nor advise you. Instead he or she will facilitate you finding your own solution at best; at worst they will help to temporarily alleviate your suffering by simply listening. Hopefully they can accomplish both. Every time a client sits in front of me, I remind myself how privileged I am to share their story and walk with them a few miles along their path. I am a baby counsellor with much to learn but I think I'm finally on the right road.

Does counselling actually work?

This is important, for clients, counsellors themselves as well as other health care professionals. Professor Mick Cooper, from the University of Strathclyde in Scotland published a wonderful book entitled "Essential research findings in counselling and psychotherapy". In it, he summarises a lot of meta-analysis of research into counselling and its efficacy. Meta-analysis involves analysing many different research studies in order to find some consensus. Here are some facts about counselling as published by Professor Cooper:

Clients who received therapy significantly improve over time when compared with control individuals suffering from the same issues but who did not access counselling.

Counselling is as effective as pharmacological treatments (drugs used to treat depression and anxiety) over the long term.

Between 10 and 20 sessions are required for 50% of clients to show clinical improvement.

Counselling and psychotherapy have been shown as the most cost effective treatments for psychological illnesses when compared with other treatment types.

Summary

This book is broken into two stand-alone sections:

In Section one you will find a brief summary of the major schools of counselling and psychotherapy.

Section two is for current students of counselling and psychotherapy.

Reading list

Essential Research Findings in Counselling and Psychotherapy: The Facts are Friendly by Mick Cooper (Sage Publications in association with BACP)

Section One:
History and Theory of Counselling and Psychotherapy

Chapter Two

Psychodynamic Theory

Psychodynamic theory comprises a number of separate psychology-based theories, devised to explain and treat mental disturbances. Its principle pioneers include Sigmund Freud, Carl Jung and Alfred Adler among others.

Psychoanalysis and Sigmund Freud

Sigmund Freud (1856-1939) was born in Vienna, the first of three boys and five girls. He eventually studied medicine but always considered himself first and foremost as a medical scientist. Freud devoted much of his life to the conception and development of what he termed, psychoanalysis.

Freud and his theories are much maligned today. He has been rendered down into a caricature, often depicted as the elderly, bearded gentleman with an over-the-top Germanic accent. His theories have been rejected as limited, not based on empirical data and largely focusing on sex as the underlying cause of all mental disturbances. His refusal to admit to himself and his peers the possibility that sex might be just one causative factor in what was termed neurosis, served to foment this stereotypical view. He seems to have been an obstinate and single-minded man, characteristics shared by many pioneers.

I must admit to sharing this stereotype of Freud prior to my studies. The fact remained that I knew little beyond this caricature. After briefly studying the man and his vast works I have a limited understanding of his theories but have also come to respect him and his work. We are in danger of throwing the baby out with the bath water when we dismiss Freud and his theories. His work must be placed in the context of his time, which was a relentlessly repressed and prudish Victorian society; sex and sexuality was a taboo subject.

Early in his career, Freud visited Paris in order to learn from the French neurologist, Jean-Martin Charcot. Charcot believed that some types of paralysis did not result from pathological lesions (disease with a physical cause such as a virus) but instead were psychosomatic, meaning they had their origin in the mind. Charcot believed that psychosomatic paralysis was associated with a hitherto forgotten trauma. He found that when his patients revisited the trauma under hypnosis, their paralysis dissipated. Freud subsequently expanded Charcot's theory beyond trauma and theorised that unpalatable thoughts or emotions as well as traumatic events were repressed by the unconscious in many people. He postulated that these repressed thoughts and emotions struggled to be released into conscious life, resulting in the development of neurotic symptoms. Freud speculated that these symptoms would be eliminated once the repressed thoughts and or emotions were revealed to the conscious mind, thereby relieving the tension between the unconscious and conscious aspects. In short, as human beings we cram our nasty ideas, feelings, impulses and wishes into the farthest and darkest part of our minds in the futile hope that they will stay there. Unbeknown to us, these unwanted aspects gnash their teeth and fight to see the light of day in our conscious world. The mental effort required to keep these thoughts at bay manifests itself in different ways: the development of an irrational fear of buttons for example or a compulsive need to lock your door 5 times or perhaps the sudden emergence of anger and sadness without any obvious cause. Freud expanded these ideas into the interpretation of dreams and developed a long lived anatomy of the mind.

Id, ego and superego - a new anatomy of the mind

Every time I read the works of Freud and his contemporaries I am amazed at the amount of words and phrases either coined by them or dragged from obscurity, that have passed into the lexicon (common speech) of our times. I doubt there is an adult in the western world that hasn't at some time come across the word ego. We use these words to imply many different things, often far removed from their intended use by the likes of Freud. So what did Freud mean by ego, and its perhaps lesser well known counterparts, the Id and super ego?

As referred to before, Freud toyed with the idea that we as human beings repress unwanted thoughts and feelings deep into our unconscious. Freud gave the title, Id to these unpalatable thoughts, wishes and impulses. The Id has often been compared to an untamed, uncivilised beast, filled with raw emotion and want.

He coined the term ego to describe the aspect of our minds which counteracts and keeps the beast or Id at bay. The ego is our waking consciousness and wants to keep the self on the straight and narrow; but where does the ego get its values from and how does it know what is straight and what is narrow in the first place?

Freud called that aspect of the mind, which educates the ego, the super ego. The super ego responds to and represents the social values and traditions of whatever community in which the self resides. In short, the Id "wants", the ego "represses" and "censors", while the super ego "polices" the whole process making sure the ego is doing its job, according to the social norms of the time (Figure 2.1). We can see already how the meaning of some of these terms such as ego has been altered over the years. The word ego today is a common euphemism for self-obsessed; selfish people are sometimes referred to as being egotistic. For Freud, the ego represented the interface between the unconscious Id and the conscious mind that includes the ego and the superego. All of these components are all about the self but perhaps should not be used to imply self-centredness.

Figure 2.1 Freud devised a new anatomy of the mind, in which the conscious **ego** tries to repress and censor the raw craving of the unconscious **id**. Meanwhile the **super-ego**, in the form of authority figures; the **super-ego** enforces societal norms and educates the ego in what thoughts and feelings to express.

Freud, sex and Oedipus Rex

Sex seemed an obvious area of study for Freud considering sexuality is associated with the physical as much as the mental. He liked the idea of neurosis having its origin in some physical part of the brain. Sex has mental components that include emotion and fantasy as well the physiological such as its connection with the hormonal and nervous systems of the body. His initial investigations into sex as a potential root cause for neurosis led him to develop the seduction theory. He speculated that neurosis was as a result of the seduction of young children by adults. Since this is a traumatic and forbidden act, Freud believed that the child would repress it, only to have the memory manifest itself in later years disguised as neurotic symptoms and hysteria.

This is a startling and shocking generalisation to make, even in the 21st century and Freud ultimately abandoned the seduction theory for three reasons. First, although sexual seduction of children by adults happened (and unfortunately continues today), it was unlikely to occur in the great frequency he was suggesting (he based this on the numbers of patients presenting to his clinic with neurotic symptoms). Secondly, he would have had to view his own father as having seduced some of Freud's siblings, who displayed neurotic and hysterical symptoms as adults. Thirdly, through self-analysis, Freud began to formalise an idea that fantasy in addition to an actual event such as erotic seduction experienced by the child, could account for mental disturbances visited upon the adult. During this analysis he realised that as a child aged 4 or 5, he himself harboured erotic feelings toward his mother; a fantasy which had a powerful impact on him once recalled. As a result, he came to the conclusion that the majority of his neurotic patients were actually hampered by erotic fantasies instead of an actual event from their childhood. These fantasies represented a type of wish fulfilment that would never be met and in some people would cause neurotic and hysterical symptoms. His conclusion: sexual fantasy and the subsequent drive for wish fulfilment by the beastly Id was as powerful as any physical act. Such fantasies were forbidden and therefore repressed. This repression led to great tension in the adult and ultimately disturbances in the psyche.

Freud's self-analysis also led him to formulate one of his most famous theories, the Oedipus (pronounced ee-di-pus) complex. Oedipus Rex or 'Oedipus the King' was written by the Greek play-write Sophocles and centres largely around Oedipus who becomes the king, accidentally murders his father as faith decrees and marries his widowed mother. It is as you might imagine a tragedy that ends badly for all concerned. Freud aligned his own experience, where he temporarily became attracted to his mother as a young boy and as a result regarded his father as a competitor, to that of Oedipus. He also observed this pattern in his patients: some male patients revealed a profound jealousy of their father's position in relation to the mother. As a result Freud decreed this temporary phase a universal and necessary experience of all young boys and girls.

The Oedipus complex the plays out as follows: As a result of the insatiable Id, a young boy becomes sexually attracted to his mother and regards his father as a competitor who must be removed. However, thanks to the sensible ego, the boy recognises that the father is more powerful physically and mentally and fears castration should he challenge him. This fear of castration (castration anxiety) eventually leads to the end of this phase and the successful development of the super ego (which acts as the child's conscience; a mental version of the father). Freud believed that each child must reconcile and bond with the parent of the same sex in order to emerge as an adult with a healthy psyche. Those who failed to accomplish this task in psychosexual development were doomed to develop neurosis in later years.

So what about girls you might ask? Freud seemed to lack even rudimentary understanding of women at times, which is borne out by his development of the female equivalent of the Oedipus complex, Penis Envy. For Freud, young girls dismissed their mothers when they realise that they do not possess a penis. They subsequently look to the father as desirable and wish to become impregnated by him in order to receive some of his power. This phase ends for girls when they realise that other men, apart from their father also possess the ability to impregnate them.

I am embarrassed just writing those last few lines. For men and women of our age, it seems preposterous that someone could formulate such a theory about female development. However, we have to put ourselves in the zeitgeist of the time. Women were regarded as inferior to men in every facet except one: their capacity to give birth to a new human being. Judged from that perspective we can see how someone of Freud's era might come to such a conclusion, no matter how unpalatable it is for those of us living in the 21st century.

It is easy, as I said earlier, to throw the baby out with the bath water where Freud is concerned. However, if we ignore such provocative terms such as castration anxiety and penis envy, as well as the unpalatable idea of being sexually attractive to one's parent, much of his theory makes sense. These developments do not have to be so dramatic nor do they have to be associated with such inflammatory terms but I think we can all see similarities in our own relationships.

Analytical Psychology and Carl Gustav Jung

The Swiss born Carl Jung (1875-1961) is perhaps the second most famous psychiatrist/psychologist of the 20th century, behind Sigmund Freud. A long-time admirer of Freud, the two developed a personal and professional relationship for several years before their infamous and acrimonious split in 1913.

Jung was a gifted but lonely child who eventually enrolled to study natural sciences and medicine at Basel University in 1885. Perhaps because (or in spite) of his father and other relatives who were members of the church, Jung developed a keen interest in theology and matters of the spirit. In psychiatry, he believed he had found the perfect marriage between the natural sciences and the spirit, both of which he loved equally. He began his apprenticeship in psychiatry at the famous Burgholzli Psychiatric Hospital in Zurich, which served to galvanise his interest in psychiatry and from which he published a paper based on the famous word-association test, originally devised by Francis Galton, an English mathematician with a strong interest in psychology. In this test the experimenter calls out words to the patient from a set list, after which the patient is asked to respond with the first word that comes to mind. The experimenter notes how long it takes for the patient to respond and makes a note of the time and the word.

Pervious researchers had noted that delayed responses were often associated with distressing or unpalatable thoughts or memories. In fact, such words were frequently clustered together with others and seemed to represent complexes of thoughts, emotions or memories. Today, we frequently use 'complex' to refer to a collection of behaviours which occur as a result of repressed trauma. Jung put two and two together and noticed that such complexes revealed by the word-association test were very similar to the repressed wishes and memories Freud had seen in his patients. He agreed with Freud that that these aspects of the psyche were repressed by the child, only to resurface as neurosis in the adult. As a result, psychoanalysis could unveil these hidden memories and free the patient from suffering. Freud responded with great interest to Jung's paper on the subject, so much so that he invited Jung to visit him in Vienna, thus sparking their friendship.

Both men acknowledged the fact that they needed each other. Freud needed an enthusiastic disciple and son, while Jung needed a father figure as erudite as himself (unlike his own father). The friendship lasted seven years and broke when Freud could no longer tolerate Jung's refusal to tow the psychoanalytical line, which stipulated that failures in psychosexual development underpinned neurosis. Likewise, Carl Jung could not accept Freud's reluctance to accept the existence of causative agents other than sex in the development of neurosis. At this time, Jung was also beginning to formulate his theory of the collective unconscious, a concept completely alien to Freud who believed the mind and its machinations began and ended with the individual.

The Collective Unconscious

Jung had many documented dreams which helped establish the platform upon which his theories were based. One of the most influential occurred in 1909 when both he and Freud were on a speaking tour of the eastern United States of America. Jung recounted this dream in his memoir "Memories, Dreams, Reflections", in which he described his exploration of a multi-storied house. The top floor was replete with modern furnishings, however, the layout of the rooms changed as he descended to the floors below. It seemed as though he was moving progressively backward in time until he eventually reached the basement where he found ancient human skulls buried in sand. For Jung, this dream represented the layers of the unconscious, found in every human being. The primordial basement with its half buried skulls suggested a collective unconscious, shared by all human beings. He proposed that this store of collective knowledge is readily available to all humans, frequently manifesting in our dreams.

Archetypes

Archetypes are the basic units of the collective human unconscious. They represent identical psychic structures common to each person. Although archetypes are common to all people, the form they take is unique to the individual and based upon his or her experiences in a social and personal context. A good example of this might be the archetype of the 'Mother'. If we are to follow Jung's theories of the collective unconscious and its components (archetypes) the archetype of the mother would play out as follows:

Infants are not born with a blank canvas or 'empty hard drive' ready for adults and the world to imprint their experiences upon it. Instead they (we) are born with certain psychical structures called archetypes. One of these archetypes is that of the mother. This maternal archetype is common to all human beings and conveys to the infant what is expected of a mother. However, the precise image of the mother archetype found in a Japanese infant might differ from an Irish one; nevertheless, the essence would remain the same. The infant's maternal archetype engages with the mothers' to assist both in the generation and maintenance of a maternal bond. For Jung, these inherited archetypes not only aid in the survival of the species but remain the source of all ideas and great discoveries that aid mankind in its evolution.

Like Freud, Jung believed that myths and legends had a great deal more to say about the human psyche than previously thought. Jung suggested that myths found around the world shared certain components or archetypes, from the developed European societies of the time to the myths of hidden and isolated tribes of the Amazon basin.

In his writings, Jung frequently recounted the story of a schizophrenic patient who told him that if he, the patient, squinted at the sun he could see a penis protruding from its side, which he understood was the origin of wind! Some years later, Jung came across the same story in Greek mythology, thousands of years old. As a result, Jung counted this experience as partial proof of a collective unconscious shared by all humans. This patient was apparently a poor,

15

uneducated man who would have never come across Greek mythology or the like in his life. Obviously there is a great deal more to Carl Jung and his Analytical Psychology than I have laid out in this limited chapter. He contributed hugely to the arena of dream interpretation as well as to our understanding of human development; unlike Freud, he wrote a great deal about the development of human beings well into their old age. Likewise, he was instrumental in the development of personality theory and coined the terms introvert and extrovert; words commonly used today to respectively describe quiet, contemplative individuals as well as their more outward-going, gregarious counterparts.

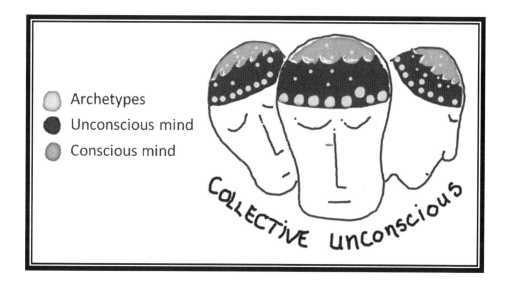

Figure 2.2. Jung theorised that all humans are born with certain universal components he called archetypes, which are part of the collective unconscious. These archetypes normally reside in the unconscious but emerge into the conscious mind when needed by the individual. Some examples of archetypes include: father, mother, male, female, healer, lover among many others. Archetypes typically manifest themselves in dreams in order to help the dreamer.

Individual psychology and Alfred Adler

Alfred Adler (1870 - 1937), was born in Vienna, the second youngest in a family of eight. As a young boy he suffered from a variety of illnesses and didn't show much promise academically. The combination of these experiences motivated him to study medicine and ultimately to found his own branch of psychodynamic theory, Individual Psychology. He was president of the Vienna Psychoanalytic Society up until his eventual split with Sigmund Freud in 1911. Freud was openly bitter and stated frequently that those who followed Adler's theories could not be taken seriously as psychiatrists.

Adler could not accept Freud's biological and deterministic view of the psyche. As we have seen, Freud believed that failure of the child to pass through the various stages of psychosexual development doomed that person to a life of neurosis. For Adler, the social environment as well as the presence of life goals played a significant role in the development of a healthy mind.

He went on to propose that feelings of inferiority in young human beings were essential for healthy development; such thoughts and emotions motivate people to succeed in life and ultimately to become more complete human beings. Although this drive toward superiority exists in all human beings, for some it is quenched because of faulty subjective perceptions. It should be noted that for Adler the word superior was not intended to mean superior in an elitist way. He used the word to imply the movement of an individual from a lower level of awareness to a higher one. This concept was taken up by other luminaries in the world of psychology such as Abraham Maslow and Carl Rogers, more of whom will be described in later chapters.

Subjective perception and the individual

According to Adler, each person, depending upon his or her social environment, as well their experiences in the first six years of life, develops a unique subjective perception (or reality). Subjective perception allows the individual to develop his or her own set of values, thoughts, beliefs, feelings and perspectives. In Individual Psychology, the psychotherapist is more interested in the client's subjective perception than the objective one. It is only through the subjective perception that the Adlerian counsellor can learn about how the client came to this juncture in their life and how to facilitate a change in their subjective perception. Adler adopted a number of systematic approaches to accomplish this task.

First of all, Adlerian counsellors place a great deal of emphasis on generating a rapport with clients. Interestingly, Adler was the first psychotherapist to abandon the psychiatrist's couch made famous by Freud, to the now very familiar 'two chair' approach, where the counsellor faces the client. While Freud often believed that the psychiatrist knew best, Adler dismissed this approach by trying to establish a more equal relationship between psychotherapist and client.

After establishing a sound relationship with the client, the Adlerian counsellor next investigates the first 6 years of life. Individual Psychology is more concerned with the present and the future; nevertheless, experiences early in life serve to shape the subjective reality of the child and so must be examined. These experiences feed in to our subjective perception of the world and serve to establish a set of core beliefs, which in turn lead us to make assumptions about ourselves and our environment.

Imagine a young woman with a hyper critical mother, who never encouraged her as a child. During these earlier years she will establish a number of core beliefs, one of which might be 'I am of no use to myself or anyone else'. This core belief subsequently leads to a number of assumptions. For example, "If I go to the party nobody will speak to me because I am useless." Adler invited such clients to examine their core beliefs and challenged the associated assumptions. It is interesting to note that modern Cognitive Behavioural Therapies (which will be discussed in subsequent chapters), examine core beliefs and assumption in order to alter distorted thinking in clients.

Motivation and drive as a result of feelings of inferiority

Once the distorted aspects of the client's subjective perception have been addressed, the Adlerian counsellor proceeds to examine current feelings of inferiority. It is the goal of the psychotherapist to facilitate the client in using such feelings to drive personal development. As we have seen, Adler believed that the evolution of human beings was as a direct result of this inherent drive to move from a position of inferiority to one of superiority. At the end of the process, the client should leave with a more balanced subjective perception as well as a newfound motivation to become a more complete human being.

Summary

- Psychodynamic theory was largely spear headed by three principle pioneers: Sigmund Freud, Carl Jung and Alfred Adler.
- Freud's psychoanalytical theory is based on the fact that each child must resolve an unconscious sexual tension with the parent of the opposite sex and reconcile with the parent of the same sex with whom he or she is unconsciously in competition. Those who fail to accomplish this task in psychosexual development are doomed to develop mental illness (neurosis) in later years.
- Jung's analytical psychology acknowledges the basic tenets of Freudian psychoanalytical theory but rejects the notion that all neurosis emerges as a result of failed psychosexual development. Jung believed that humans are in touch with a collective unconscious which has as a great an impact on the individual as external events and relationships. This collective unconscious contains themes called archetypes that help humans develop psychically and spiritually. Unlike Freud, Jung placed great emphasis on spirituality in the development of the human psyche.
- Adler was a disciple of Freud, who went on to develop individual psychology. The core tent of this psychology holds that a child's inherent feelings of inferiority in the developmental stage provide the requisite tension to strive for superiority in later life. This tension underpins human development and evolution. Adlerian counsellors facilitate the client in using such feelings of inferiority to drive personal development.

Reading list

- Freud: A Very Short Introduction by Anthony Storr

- Jung: A Very Short Introduction by Anthony Stevens

- Memories, Dreams, Reflections by Carl Jung

- The Individual Psychology of Alfred Adler: A Systematic Presentation in Selections from His Writings, edited by Heinz L. Ansbacher and Rowena R. Ansbacher

- Theory and Practice of Counseling and Psychotherapy by Gerald Corey

Chapter Three
Humanistic Schools of Psychotherapy

The beginnings of humanistic counselling and psychotherapy in the 20th Century

From the 1950's onward, the world was gradually exposed to the emergence of a very new type of psychotherapy that differed greatly from the established psychodynamic model of the time. These new therapeutic approaches were pioneered by a disparate and visionary group of therapists that included Abraham H. Maslow, Carl R. Rogers and Viktor Frankl among others, and are now collectively termed Humanistic therapies. At the core of humanistic counselling lies the person and humanistic psychotherapists believe that the ultimate goal of therapy is for the person to reach his or her full potential as a human being. To use a humanistic term (first coined by the German psychiatrist Kurt Goldstein), the person must strive for self–actualisation.

Abraham Maslow

Abraham H. Maslow (1908 – 1970) was an American psychologist whose impact stretches from the world of psychology to business. Maslow expanded on Goldstein's idea of self-actualisation and made it a principle tenet of his new humanistic style of counselling. He found that certain people (starting with two of his beloved university teachers) shared common traits that made them appear more grounded and psychologically healthy than others. According to Maslow, self-actualised individuals shared eight common attributes or needs which required the person to take responsibility for their lives and to be honest and open to their own intuition and above all to follow their own path. Unlike the psychodynamic analysts who came before him, Maslow argued that the person has it within him or herself to 'self actualise' and neither requires the therapist to be a "helper nor a teacher".

The eight characteristics of self-actualised people

1. Experience reality fully, without the self-consciousness of an adolescent.
2. Every day we make choices, which will either be safe and non-dynamic or those that hold fear and potentially lead to growth. Those who chose growth are self-actualised.
3. Listen to hunches and intuition as opposed to those in authority and the established norm.
4. Be honest and take responsibility.
5. Be courageous and prepared to be disliked for their opinions.
6. Engage in hard work; constantly striving to be the best he or she can be.
7. Peak experiences – Maslow believed these experiences happen to everyone but few recognise them for what they are. They might be described as flashes of intuition or of a universal truth that change the life of the person for the good.
8. Self-actualised people actively seek out who they are inside. They break their psyche down into its various constituents, especially the unpalatable ones. They focus particularly on their defences, in order to break them down.

Maslow's human psychology and counselling

Maslow railed against the medicalised model of psychotherapy:

"I have used the words therapy, psychotherapy, patient. Actually, I hate all these words and I hate the medical model that they imply because the medical model suggests that the person who comes to the counsellor is sick, beset by disease and illness and seeking a cure."
(The farther reaches of human nature, page 49).

He firmly believed that the person has it within to self-actualise and merely requires the counsellor to reflect his or her help, as well as providing a little support along the way. The counsellor doesn't reach down to help the 'patient' up from his lofty position. Neither is the counsellor a teacher, since self-actualisation involves intrinsic learning whereby the individual already knows the answers.

Hierarchy of human needs

Maslow is perhaps more famous in the 21st century in business management circles, due to the pervasive nature of his hierarchy of human needs, which can be found on university syllabi all over the world. Maslow suggested that human beings have basic needs that change as the needs below are met. This hierarchy is particularly relevant today when we see the great gulf in wealth between citizens of the so called developed world versus those living in the developing world. The hierarchy is illustrated in figure 3.1. and includes the following needs:

- Physiological needs: food, water, air, sleep and sex
- Safety in the form of freedom from fear and anxiety
- The need to belong and be loved
- Self-esteem
- Need for self-actualisation - need to know and understand the world in which he or she lives in

The starving individual is unlikely to be concerned with self-esteem issues, likewise those who live in violent societies care little about self-actualisation. These needs are very apparent when we consider the malaise of the western world, whose citizens suffer what might be referred to as 'first world problems', where depression as a result of lack of self-esteem or meaning in life is commonplace.

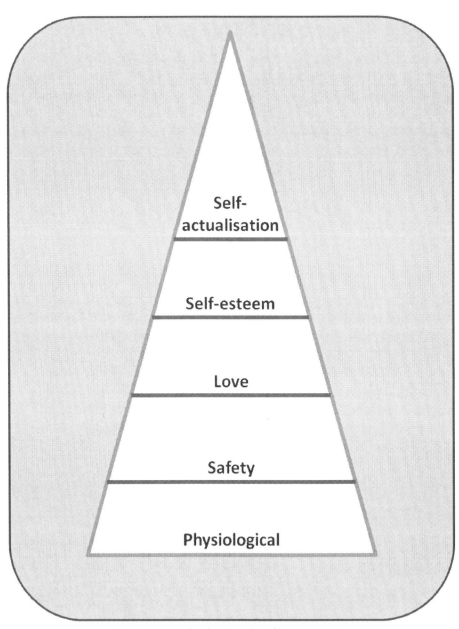

Figure 3.1. Maslow's hierarchy of human needs.

Person-centred Therapy and Carl Rogers

Carl Rogers (1902 - 1987) was an American psychologist and psychotherapist who started off life with the intention of becoming a Christian minister. However, he soon became interested in psychology. He subsequently worked at the Child Study Department at the University of Rochester, New York State. It was during his time there as a clinical psychologist that he encountered a woman and her son who was attending Roger's department because of serious behavioural issues. Based on her case report, Rogers felt that the boy's mother was at the root of the problem; she appeared to have rejected the child at a young age. Rogers tried to impress upon the mother the reason for her son's behaviour but without success. Eventually, he gave up and they agreed to part. On her way out, she asked if he (Rogers) ever counselled adults. He said he did and the woman sat back down and began to relate her story to him. This represented a watershed moment for Rogers. The woman revealed a troubled relationship with her husband as well as a personal sense of failure and confusion. Rogers revealed later that it was not he as counsellor, but the client who knew best. He had made serious assumptions about her as a patient, based on a sterile case report. He realised that since the client knew how to cure herself, there was no need for the therapist to interject and show the way. The counsellor's role was merely to facilitate the client in bringing about their own change.

The urge to fix

Rogers believed that the more he was open to the realities within himself, the less likely he was to rush in and fix the client. This he found could lead to profound change in both the counsellor and the client. In essence, Rogers moved from asking "How can I fix and treat this patient?" to "How can I provide a relationship, which this person may use for personal growth?"

The facilitation of personal growth and the characteristics of a helping relationship

As far as Rogers was concerned, techniques and tricks of the trade were only a temporary fix that would ultimately fail. For him, if one could foster a genuine relationship with the client by being honest and real, then the client had a good chance of recovery. Rogers provides an example as to how this might work in real life, based on a study of schizophrenics engaged in therapy. In this study, schizophrenic patients were divided into two groups: (A) where patients demonstrated significant improvement and (B) in which patient's behaviour remained unchanged. The characteristics associated with the successful therapy provided to group A were subsequently examined and found to include the following:

- The physicians saw the patients as people as opposed to merely case studies.
- The physicians worked toward goals, set according to the patient's personality.
- Strong therapeutic relationship.

As a result of his own clinical experience as well as research studies carried out by other groups at the time, Rogers began to formulate the basic characteristics of successful and unsuccessful therapy.

Successful therapy:

- Trust
- Being understood
- Independence to make own choices

Unsuccessful therapy:

- Lack of interest on therapist's behalf
- Therapist provides advice

Interestingly, Rogers noted that the characteristics of successful therapy were independent of the type of psychotherapy on offer.

The seven stages in the process of becoming a person

Human beings who are engaged in self-actualisation (becoming more fully human) move from a fixed, objective and rigid point of non-ownership (issues are caused by others only) to a point where they express themselves in a state of continuous change, where they take responsibility for their life and acknowledge their subjective emotions. For Rogers, all people must progress through seven stages of development along this journey of self-discovery:

1. There is a blockage of internal communication and the client will not come voluntarily to therapy. The ways in which he or she experiences the present moment is fixed and based on the past. He does not communicate about internal goings on; only external events are discussed. He perceives himself as having no problems.

2. Expression begins about non-self topics such as sudden realisations about past relationships, but problems are with others and the client believes he is not responsible for them, e.g. "I thought the problems with my family were down to my father but I'm beginning to see that my mother had a role to play too. I can't believe that both of my parents have contributed to how badly I feel today." Clients who come voluntarily to therapy can sometimes be at this stage.

3. Client describes present feelings and explores the self as an object. The majority of clients actively seeking therapy are at this stage. e.g. "I need to learn how to remain calm when my parents provoke me." There is more discussion as to how the client feels about his current relationships but the emphasis remains on past relationships. Emotions remain external.

4. There is an increased differentiation of feelings as well as recognition of contradictions e.g. "I have feelings of love and hatred for my father." There is a general acceptance that problems exist and a hint that although uncomfortable, these contrasting and paradoxical feelings might be tolerated.

5. A realisation emerges that the client has contributed to his or her own problems. e.g. "I didn't always behave like an angel in the past; sometimes I started the fights myself, out of sheer petulance."

6. Gradually, a sense of self-responsibility emerges for his problems. e.g. "I could have communicated with my dad more instead of always just reacting to him. I never gave

him any allowance for the difficulties he was having outside the family when I was a kid. I didn't regard him as a person. I was focused on my needs only."

7. Finally, the person lives his problems subjectively, feeling responsible for the contributions he has made in the development of these problems. "I recognise that I have a role to play in all of my relationships with others and that I am responsible for my behaviour. I cannot control how others treat me but I can control how I react to them."

It must be noted that these stages represent a continuum, whereby the individual can be primarily at stage one but display characteristics of a higher or lower stage, under certain circumstances. It is a fluid process, often involving two steps forward and one step back, which all humans must progress through, if they are to live full lives. Self-actualisation is almost an impossible super human goal that can only be aspired to, but it is in the struggle to aspire that we become more fully human.

The core conditions of Person-centred therapy

Rogers believed that if these conditions are met then the counsellor can facilitate change in the client. The counsellor neither teaches nor advises the client, he or she merely provides the right conditions for change.

Facing the problem
The client must agree that a problem exists. Since the client is at the centre of person centred therapy, he or she must recognise the problem. The person-centred therapist will not point out a problem, unlike other types of counsellors.

Congruence
The therapist must not hide behind a veil; she must be genuine and honest with herself and with the client.

Unconditional positive regard
The counsellor must maintain a warm and caring posture, regardless of whether the client is discussing negative or positive events. The counsellor must accept the client as being a separate person with unique feelings and experiences. Like most of the core conditions, this is not always easy to maintain.

Empathic understanding
Empathy occurs when the counsellor can sense the client's fear, anger and confusion as if it was her own, without her own anger and fear becoming bound up with it.

The client must understand and feel that the counsellor is offering congruence, unconditional positive regard and empathy.
This is a crucial final condition. There isn't much point in maintaining the core conditions of person centred therapy at considerable personal effort, if the client doesn't feel accepted, safe and heard. For Rogers, when these conditions are met change will occur in the client.

Criticisms of Person-centred therapy

You should know that person-centred therapy tends to divide student and practicing counsellors alike. Person-centred therapists are often mocked for being too parrot-like. The classic stereotype of such therapists is one where the counsellor merely repeats what the client just said.

Rogers found the same process occurring in one to one therapy, group therapy, in workshops for counsellors, education and even in politics, namely that of the inherent drive in the individual, group or organisation to evolve into something new and better than before. He believed that if you provided the right conditions, growth would occur, providing the counsellor or program leader did not direct the change. This laissez-faire attitude infuriated many people. There is one account of a person-centred workshop led by Rogers where he gave the group no direction, no title for the workshop and remained silent except when asked a question. This behaviour incensed many within the group who demanded to be led. The workshop was spread over a number of days and by the second day the group spontaneously generated a topic of interest which evoked significant learning and insight for all concerned. All of the participants admitted via feedback sheets that they felt confused, anxious, let down and angry by the lack of focus and leadership but admitted that they would never have come up with such concepts had they been led by a workshop leader. Somehow the group evolved together and created something that would have been unlikely as individuals. Rogers merely facilitated these groups.

The process of person-centred therapy has been criticised for being too slow, compared with other forms of therapy and more expensive as a result. Some clients can become frustrated with the lack of direction and progress. Furthermore, many clients find it very disconcerting during the first few sessions, when the counsellor just sits there smiling, waiting for the client to speak; it can be deeply uncomfortable for someone who has never been to counselling before.

One final criticism of Rogers and his theory is that it is based on the ideal that every human is good at heart no matter how unspeakable their deeds. Given the right conditions Rogers believed that this goodness would rise to the top. Critics have claimed that this is naive thinking, which gives no allowance for genuinely evil people. I will leave it for you to decide who is right and who is wrong.

Conclusion on Person-centred therapy

You can see Person-centred counselling in action, including Carl Rogers himself on YouTube. I particularly recommend a documentary made in the 1960s whereby person-centred therapy (Carl Rogers), rational emotive behavioural therapy (Albert Ellis) and gestalt therapy (Fritz Perls) were showcased by using the one client, "Gloria". This is a famous and sometimes controversial documentary that is definitely worth the view. If you would like to read more on Rogers, I recommend his book "On Becoming a Person". If you would like to see how Person-centred therapy has progressed into the 21st century then you should read anything by Brian Thorne and Dave Mearnes.

Rogers applied his core conditions well beyond counselling. He made significant contributions to education and politics, and was nominated for the Nobel peace prize for his work in South Africa and Northern Ireland. However, his lasting influence will always be on counselling. While not many therapists practice 'pure' person centred therapy, most will probably tell you that they practice cognitive behavioural therapy or gestalt therapy on a strong foundation of Rogers' core conditions.

Viktor Frankl and Logotherapy

Viktor Frankl, (1905 – 1997) was an Austrian psychiatrist who survived the death camp at Auschwitz during World War Two. A practicing psychiatrist before the war, the indescribable horrors he faced at Auschwitz led him to form the basis of a new psychotherapy he called logotherapy. Logos can be defined as "meaning" and Logotherapy is counselling dedicated to kindling meaning or purpose in the client.

Frankl noticed that those camp prisoners who had an external factor to focus upon, such as a family member or a significant goal, tended to survive longer than those prisoners who appeared hopeless, without anything to fix onto. Frankl's focus was a book he was writing before his capture; he sewed his manuscript into his coat in order to avoid detection. This manuscript held his focus and he continued to develop his theories throughout his time in the concentration camp. Some years after his liberation he wrote his famous book "Man's Search for Meaning", the first half of which provided an account of his experiences at Auschwitz, while the second half concerned his theories on Logotherapy.

Logotherapy

Frankl suggested that the struggle to find meaning is the primary motivating force in man; lack of meaning causes existential frustration. Therefore, the goal of the logotherapist is to help the client discover the purpose of his or her life. As with person-centred therapy, in logotherapy the client holds all the answers and not the therapist. To quote Frankl:

> *"There is nothing in life.....that would so effectively help one survive even the worst conditions, as the knowledge that there is meaning in this life."*

(Viktor Frankl, Man's Search for Meaning, pg 109).

For Frankl, the inner drive to find meaning in our lives prompts us to live active lives full of purpose; failure to do this can lead to mental illness. Frankl frequently quoted the great existential philosopher Friedrich Nietzsche, who claimed that:

> *"He who has a why to live can bear almost any now."*

Another of Frankl's quotes sums up his philosophy on life and leaves us clues as to how to recover from depression due to a lack of meaning:

"Live life as if you were living for the second time and as if you had acted the first time as wrongly as you are about to act now."

Sunday Neurosis

Have you ever had a period in your life where you felt restless or frustrated for no apparent reason on your weekends off? Frankl called this Sunday neurosis and believed it to be one of the new afflictions of modern 20th century man (in the western world). He described this neurosis as a type of depression that comes about when the individual realises there is an inherent lack of meaning in his or her life. The rush of the busy week leaves a void and the silence within becomes deafening. Many people have and continue to fill this void with alcohol or other drugs, sex, violence, relentless striving to earn money, gambling and other obsessions.

Frankl found that if he could help people find meaning and purpose he could inhibit this type of neurosis. He noted that the void left by lack of purpose could not be filled by any abstract concept but must instead be filled with a unique, specific, concrete venture, more akin to vocation.

Self-actualisation and self-transcendence

Frankl diverges from Maslow and Rogers regarding the ability of the person to self-actualise. He believed that self-actualisation was not directly attainable, since the more a person strives for it the more it would be missed. It's like trying to catch a bar of soap in the bath - the more you grasp for it, the harder it is to catch hold of! However, he did believe that self-actualisation could be acquired as a bi-product of self-transcendence.

Self-transcendence

Self-transcendence, in terms of Logotherapy occurs when the individual forgets his or her self by giving the self to a cause or to another human being. This renders the individual more human; the more human a person becomes the closer he or she comes to self-actualisation. It has long since been acknowledged that volunteering in charities that are dedicated to plight of the vulnerable can help stave off depression. By concentrating on the plight of those less fortunate than you, places life in perspective and helps take the focus from your own negative, endlessly cycling thoughts to other people in need.

The principle Therapeutic Techniques of Logotherapy

Paradoxical Intention

Frankl commented many times on the failure of psychodynamic therapies to treat certain debilitating fears. He believed that realistic fears such as the fear of death could not be "tranquillised away" by psychodynamic interpretation; neither could neurotic fears such as agoraphobia (fear of open or public spaces) be cured by philosophical understanding.

Frankl noticed that his patients often engaged in hyper-intention in relation to a fear or worry. For example, he noticed that those suffering insomnia would often try very hard to "will" themselves to sleep, thereby engaging in an exhaustive battle of concentration with the fear, frequently without success. As a result Frankl proposed 'Paradoxical Intention' as a solution to this problem.

In the second part of his book, 'Mans Search for Meaning', Frankl provided a humorous example regarding the power of paradoxical intention. He recounts the story of a young doctor who upon meeting his boss on the street began to sweat profusely. Thereafter, the man suffered excessive seating in anticipation of similar meetings. Frankl encouraged this man to resolve to SWEAT MORE the next time he experienced anticipatory fear about his excessive sweating. The next time the patient noticed fear rising within, he said to himself:

"I only sweated out a litre before, but now I'm going to pour out at least ten litres!"

The result was that after four years of suffering this embarrassing phobia, he never sweated to the same extent again. Paradoxical intention has been successful in treating anxiety, obsessive compulsive thoughts and phobias. Much of the effort concerning phobias and anxiety goes into trying to revisit and deflect them. This seems to reinforce the patterns in our brains and makes it even more difficult to adjust. Paradoxical intention by using humour and often ridiculous exaggeration places a distance between ourselves and our fears and seems to allow for new brain patterns to develop.

Hyper-reflection and its solution: de-reflection

Over-thinking is a common aspect of anxiety, depression and many phobias. These thoughts become intertwined with the negative emotions and we become locked in place. De-reflection is a deliberate switch of focus from the self to something external. By doing this we not only change focus but enhance our perspective on the problem we were reflecting on.

Conclusion on logotherapy

Logotherapy is concerned with the search for meaning. The logotherapist helps facilitate this search, all the time knowing that the client has the answers within. I have found much in Logotherapy that has helped me in my endeavours to become a better person and counsellor. I recommend reading Viktor Frankl's book "Man's Search for meaning" as well as those of perhaps his most famous successor, Irvin Yalom. Yalom has published a number of wonderful and readable books on Logotherapy and counselling in general.

Gestalt therapy

According to the German-born Fritz Perls (1893 – 1970), Ralph Hefferline and Paul Goodman, the Gestalt outlook is the original, undistorted, natural approach to life. Perls was a psychoanalyst who along with his wife Laura (also a psychoanalyst) helped develop Gestalt therapy (loosely based on Gestalt psychology) in response to the inadequacies they found with psychoanalysis.

The central thesis of Gestalt therapy suggests that modern man has lost this original and untainted 'wholeness'; he is split into numerous components as result of his interaction with society and his environment. People view their environment in terms of contrasts: body and mind, organism and environment. As a result, Gestalt therapy seeks to re-integrate the person and render him whole once again. Gestalt is a German word that has no direct translation in English. Depending on the context, It can mean: form, shape, whole, configuration, structure and theme. It is probably easiest to understand Gestalt therapy as a holistic approach to re-integration, which unlike psychodynamic therapy includes body, mind and soul.

Figure and Background

When we experience our environment we don't fully see everything in one single panoramic view. We are usually only aware of one specific aspect within our field of vision; this is called our point of contact or in Gestalt terms, the *figure*. Everything else that remains outside of our awareness can be called the *background* (or ground). This perception of what becomes *figure* and *background* is dynamic and changes constantly. It is best illustrated by the classic Gestalt images of the hag/girl and the vase/faces composites, seen in Figures 3.2. and 3.3. respectively. If you look at Figure 3.2. you will either see an old woman or a young elegant woman. In fact, your perception of what is *background* and what is the main *figure* might change as you stare at the image. The same can be said of Figure 3.3., where either a vase (or sometimes also referred to as a candlestick holder) or two faces in profile, appear as the principle *figure*.

In Gestalt therapy, what you perceive as the central *figure* depends on your past experiences, beliefs, values, prejudices and preferences. For example, if you suffered at the hands of a harsh grandmother as a child you might see the old hag as the *background* with the image of the young girl in the foreground, acting as the *figure* (Figure 5.2.). As you can see form this example, the *background* provides the context in which the figure (central point of your awareness) is observed. Your dislike of the old woman might be unconsciously directing you to focus on a more positive image such as that of the young girl. Of course, you might also be aware of your reasons for choosing the young girl as the *figure* of your awareness. The unconscious focusing on one image at the expense of the other (e.g. old versus young woman) has been linked to the Freudian concept of repressed memories and wishes. Gestalt therapists facilitate a change in your awareness by urging clients to swap figure and background as well as experimenting with what each means to them. It is though that this process serves to unite those aspects of the client that have become separate as a result of past experiences. The goal is similar to that of self-actualisation, with a particular focus on changing perception as a means to complete integration.

Figure 3.2. Gestalt image simultaneously depicting a young and old woman.

Figure 3.3. Gestalt image simultaneously depicting a vase and two faces in profile.

Experimentation and Gestalt therapy

The Gestalt therapist doesn't place demands upon the client i.e. you need to relax, pull yourself together, you should forgive etc. Such demands only enhance neurosis. Instead the therapist suggests a series of graded experiments during sessions. These experiments are repeated and the client is asked each time to describe any thoughts or emotions that emerge during the session. The task results are not important; instead the client gleans information from ideas, emotions or memories that interfere with the experiment.

Daniel Rosenblatt published a book in 1976 entitled 'The Gestalt Therapy Primer'. It is a small book that contains a number of experiments which serve to illustrate what Gestalt therapy is like. The reader is encouraged to participate in each experiment.

A final word of caution

I have recommended a particular YouTube video in the section of Person-centred therapy, which involves a lady called Gloria, who is subjected to three different types of therapy: Person-centred therapy, Gestalt and Rational-emotive behavioural therapy (REBT). Fritz Perls is the Gestalt therapist in this video. In it, he is aggressive and sometimes rude to Gloria. Further reading on the internet provides more evidence of his bad behaviour. The result is that Gestalt and Fritz Perls in particular appear unpalatable for some people. Please don't let this example of Gestalt therapy put you off reading more on the subject. From what I believe, it is just one example that is not particularly representative of modern Gestalt therapy.

Do Humanistic therapies work?

Meta-analyses of many separate studies carried out on humanistic counselling show that they are very effective forms of therapy; just as effective as psychodynamic approaches. Person-centred therapy has been shown to have the strongest impact on adults and children with mild or moderate depression. Likewise, Gestalt therapy has been found to be very effective for relieving symptoms of depression, mild phobias and other psychological difficulties (Essential Research Findings in Counselling and psychotherapy by Professor Mick Cooper).

Summary

- Humanistic therapy came about in response to the medicalised approach of psychodynamic therapy at the time.

- Humanistic counselling puts the client in the driving seat and facilitates him or her to aspire to self-actualisation (this is the ultimate goal of some humanistic modalities, whereby the client is facilitated to aspire to his or her full potential as a human being).

- Person-centred therapy, devised by Carl Rogers is based on three core principles: unconditional positive regard, empathic understanding and congruence. Person-centred therapy is a non-directive form of therapy that assumes the client already has all the tools required to become healthy again.

- Viktor Frankl's logotherapy postulates that much of human neurosis is due to a lack of meaning and purpose. Once a person seeks and finds meaning, he or she will indirectly move toward self-actualisation.

- Gestalt is a German word with no direct English translation but generally accepted to imply wholeness. Gestalt therapy is collaborative; clients are urged to engage in experiments which rearrange the foreground and background of various internal beliefs about oneself and the environment.

Reading list

- The Farther Reaches of Human Nature by Abraham Maslow

- The 100 most eminent psychologists of the 20th century by Steven Haggbloom. *Review of General Psychology*, 2002, vol. 6 (2) 139-152.)

- On Becoming a Person: A Therapist's View of Psychotherapy by Carl Rogers

- Man's search for meaning by Viktor Frankl

- The Gestalt Therapy Primer by Daniel Rosenblatt

Chapter Four
Cognitive Behavioural Therapies

Cognitive behavioural therapies (CBT) are very different from either the psychodynamic or humanistic schools of psychotherapies. They largely emerged from the scientific behavioural studies of the 1940s and 1950s, which experimented on both animal and human behaviour. Those who practice cognitive therapies refer to the fact that there have been more scientific studies carried out in this area of psychotherapy than in all the other schools combined. They are mostly practical, logical, brief and require a great deal of participation by the client in his or her recovery. Many practitioners of this school are more directive; cognitive-based counsellors often act as educators who collaborate with clients in the correction of their faulty thinking, which they believe lead to disturbed emotion and behaviour. Today, cognitive therapies are being adopted by health services all over the world and are viewed by the medical profession and other health sectors as a cheaper, quicker and more efficient means of dealing with depression, obsessive compulsive disorder, eating disorders and anxiety.

CBT is divided into three waves; the first of which was based on the behavioural research carried out by psychologists such as B.F. Skinner, in the mid-20th century. This behavioural psychology was subsequently added to and enhanced by the pioneers of the second wave, who emerged during the second half of the 20th century and include William Glasser, Albert Ellis and Aaron Beck. The third wave began in the 1980s and continues to flourish in the 21st century. Third wave modalities include Acceptance and Commitment therapy (ACT), Schema therapy, Mindfulness-based Cognitive therapy (MBCT), among others. All of this implies a dynamic and exciting field of psychotherapy.

Choice Theory and Reality Therapy

William Glasser (born in 1925) is an American psychiatrist who devised Reality therapy in the 1950s in response to what he saw as the inefficient and ineffective psychodynamic approaches to 'curing' mental illness. Glasser has battled all his life, but particularly in his earlier years against the medical establishment; his theories have evoked vehement criticism from traditional psychiatrists. He shuns medical diagnoses and the labelling of people (e.g. clinically depressed or schizophrenic), which he believes are harmful and largely irrelevant. He has said that such labels should be used for insurance purposes only. Glasser also believes that the only types of real mental illnesses are those with a biological origin, where there is damage to the brain, as a result of physical injury or genetic-based disease. For Glasser, those people with 'mental' illnesses should be referred to a neurologist (doctors that deal with the brain and central nervous system) and not psychiatrists. He has written much about the potential damage caused to patients by the ubiquitous use of medication to treat mental disturbances.

Choice Theory

Glasser devised Choice Theory in the 1980s in an attempt to explain how Reality therapy works. Like Maslow, Glasser suggested that humans are born with basic needs, which include: survival, love and belonging, power or purpose, freedom and fun.

In Choice theory it is proposed that when we feel bad, one or more of these needs is not being met. Glasser also believed that these needs are highly dependent on our relationships with other human beings; as a consequence, inability to maintain healthy relationships leads to deterioration in mental health. Unlike other psychotherapists, Glasser suggests that it is the individual who is responsible for how bad he or she feels. Instead of feeling depressed, implying some external force caused this bad feeling, the person is actually '*depressing*' him or herself. This concept can be extended to *headaching*, *angering* and *anxieting*[1] among other actions. In other words, we make ourselves depressed, angry or anxious, as a result of bad relationships with others, which prevent one or more of our basic needs from being met.

Core aspects of choice theory and Reality Therapy

Choice and responsibility

Reality therapists encourage clients to ignore those aspects of relationships and life which are out of their control. Instead, clients are asked to focus on what is within their circle of influence, particularly their thoughts, emotions and subsequent behaviour. Clients are urged to **choose** for themselves how to feel and behave.

Focus on the present

You normally won't hear a Reality therapist dwelling on the past, as you might with practitioners of other types of psychotherapy. Choice theory and Reality therapy is focused primarily on present behaviour and how to change it. Unhealthy focusing on the past prevents clients from taking responsibility for their present behaviour.

---

[1] Obviously words such as 'anxieting' aren't real words we use in everyday language. Glasser turned words like anger and anxiety into verbs to imply that we impose these feelings upon ourselves.

Remove the focus from symptoms

Bad relationships prevent us from fulfilling our basic needs. We subsequently don the role of victim and choose unconsciously to depress, make ourselves anxious or activate pain in the body. We use these symptoms to avoid the core issue, which is to reflect upon the behaviour that led to this bad relationship in the first place. The Reality therapist ignores these symptoms and encourages clients to get to the nub of the issue quickly. Importantly, clients are asked not to focus on any prior medical diagnoses.

The therapeutic relationship

Like many humanistic forms of psychotherapy, Reality therapy also places a great deal of emphasis on establishing a good relationship between client and therapist. The client is unlikely to adopt what can seem at first, a harsh and often counterintuitive therapy if he or she does not trust the therapist. This is an important point, since critics often comment on the apparent lack of empathy between Reality therapists and their clients.

The quality world and how to achieve it

Reality therapists will ask you to reveal your ideal world and your position in it. Unrealistic aspects of this world are highlighted and rejected, while the realistic aspirations are examined in more detail. Next, the counsellor will ask the client to discuss current difficult relationships and how they are preventing the client's needs from being met. The client's behaviour is examined forensically; he or she is forced to answer the question "Is your current behaviour likely to help you achieve your quality world?" If the answer is "no", then the client is asked how their behaviour might be changed in order to help attain their goals. The client realises that he or she can **choose** to change her role in these relationships. She or he can **choose** to alter their behaviour and stop *depressing, anxieting* or *angering* and learn to take responsibility from those aspects of their lives that are within their control. Once the client accepts these concepts of Reality therapy they are ready to formulate a plan of action.

Planning

Plans don't always work out but it is important to devise them in order to move forward. If a particular plan of action fails, the counsellor and client collaborate to devise another.

The principle aspects of a good plan

Simple

Elaborate plans are almost certainly doomed to failure. Simple plans are easier to follow and their goals easier to achieve. As a result, the client feels better, stronger and in more control. Little successes lead to increasing confidence and big successes.

Attainable

The attainability of the goal must be decided between the counsellor and client. Smaller, more attainable goals enhance confidence.

Measurable

It's important for the client to be able to see his or her accomplishment in real time. Different plans have different read outs or results that can be measured.

Immediate

Plans with more long term effects are harder to maintain; clients need to see the fruit of their hard work sooner and frequently.

Controlled by the planner

Plans should be dependent on the client only and not on others, such as family members and significant others (including the counsellor!). This prevents other external factors derailing the plan and upsetting the client. Although the client must be committed and apply the plan daily, the counsellor must impress upon him or her that to slip up from time to time is human. If the client fails to make progress then the counsellor must sit down and re-evaluate the plan and course of action.

Concluding comments on Reality therapy and Choice theory

Whether you believe in Choice theory and Reality therapy or not, I think you'll find that this approach to planning is good common sense and one that we could all apply to our own aims and objectives in life. As I said at the start, Glasser's Reality Therapy has been denounced by psychiatrists. It has also been harshly criticised by humanistic counsellors as being too directive and severe on the client. Other psychotherapists have rejected the idea that clients subject themselves to severe debilitating depression or pain, as nonsense. As with all other types of psychotherapy, it is up to you to decide what works for you and your clients. Like Freud, I don't think we should throw the baby out with the bath water where Choice theory is concerned; it has a number of admirable qualities that have been shown to be effective in treating depression and anxiety.

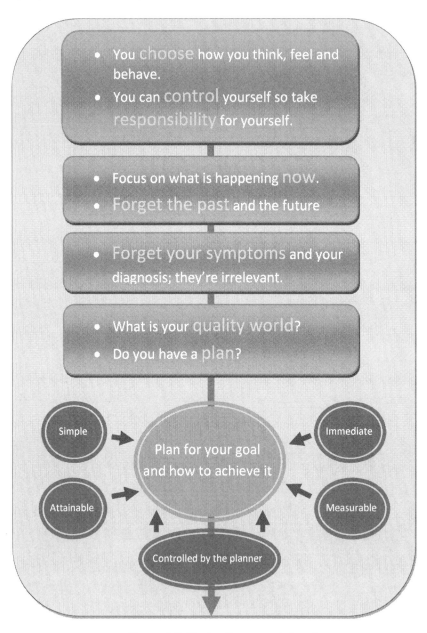

Figure 4.1. Choice theory and planning

Rational Emotive Behaviour Therapy (REBT)

Albert Ellis (1913 - 2007) was a New York-based American psychologist who went on to develop a more rational and empirically verifiable (by using experiments and scientific methods) psychotherapy. He was an avid reader of the philosophy of the east and west and the following quotes from Roman and Greek philosophers encompass Ellis's view of metal suffering and the subsequent development of a more rational psychotherapy:

"If you are distressed by anything external, the pain is not due to the thing itself but to your own estimate of it; and this you have the power to revoke at any moment."

Marcus Aurelius (Roman Emperor, first century A.D.)

"For freedom is not acquired by satisfying yourself with what you desire, but by destroying your desire."

Epictetus (Greek stoic philosopher, first century A.D.)

Like Glasser, Ellis believed that people contributed (consciously or unconsciously) to their own suffering by how they interpreted events and their relationships with others. He also suggested that we can choose not to suffer and instead take positive steps to change our behaviour. According to the basic principles of REBT, emotional disturbance (which Freud called neurosis), has its origins in cognitive, emotive and behavioural sources; neurosis is not **caused** by thoughts or cognition but simply made worse by them. Those of us with emotional disturbances establish fixed internal dogmas and have irrational expectations about how life and other human beings must treat them. Thoughts associated with such beliefs are often associated with words like *must, should* and *ought*.

The ABC model

The principle instrument of the REBT therapist is the ABC model; it is used to help clients understand the development of emotional disturbance and how they can be eliminated. Praised for its simplicity and efficiency, the ABC model consists of three interlinking components: A (activating events), B (beliefs), and C (consequences).

A - Activating event
Throughout the course of our lives we encounter events that block our desires for life.

B – Beliefs
Beliefs are divided into rational and irrational ones. Normally, activating events that serve to disturb us interact with our irrational beliefs and lead to a change in behaviour.

C – Consequences
Activating events engage internal irrational beliefs, which subsequently alter behaviour. This change in behaviour normally has a number of negative consequences that feed back into the cycle of disturbed emotion and thoughts.

Although the ABC model might seem simple, the real world scenario involves many activating events that interact with a number of rational and irrational beliefs which alters behaviour throughout the average day. These behaviours lead to more events and the cycle begins again. To make matters more complex, our countless personal ABC cycles constantly interact with those of others.

Even though REBT is a present-focused therapy it does acknowledge that we often acquire these irrational beliefs from significant others in childhood, such as parents and other authority figures. As previously described, these irrational beliefs subsequently acquire words like *should*, *must* and *ought*. REBT encourages clients to move from these dogmatic '*musts*' to what is '*preferable*'. The goal is to change thinking from "*must*" to "*prefer*".

Example:

Unhelpful thinking - "I **must** be a good counsellor all the time."

Healthy thinking - "I **prefer** to be a good counsellor but I realise that this won't always be the case."

For Ellis, irrational beliefs fall under three general categories:

1. I **must** perform well and win the approval of peers and those in authority or else I will be a worthless failure.

2. People **must** be nice and fair to me at all times otherwise they are unjust and nasty.

3. The environment I live in _must_ be safe, comfortable and advantageous; if it is not then the place I live in is horrible and life is hardly worth living.

According to Ellis, when we fall under this type of thinking, we:

"*Catastrophize, awfulize, overgneralize, personalise, jump to invalid conclusions, use emotional reasoning, dichotomize, damn themselves and others, and make other major unrealistic, anti-empirical, often false inferences and attributions.*"
(Rational emotive behaviour therapy: a reader by Albert Ellis, page 5).

That's quite a list I'm sure you'll agree. I often engage in such thinking and have had all of the above irrational beliefs rattling around in my head at some point. I believe that this type of irrational or erroneous thinking is commonplace. REBT urges clients to pay attention to thoughts and beliefs and see how they can have a direct impact on behaviour.

As a personal experiment, try to write down how many times (over the next 24 hour period) you have a thought that falls under one of the three categories outlined above. Keep a watchful eye for *oughts*, *shoulds* and *musts*. Once you notice how often you really think like this, you will find that you have the capacity to ignore the thought; in Reality theory parlance, you can **choose** not to act on these thoughts. With practice, you should be able to slowly chip away your irrational beliefs and form new, more rational and healthy ones.

Extending the ABC model

Later on in the development of REBT therapy, Ellis added two extra steps to the ABC model: D (disputing) and E (effective new philosophy).

D – Disputing

In much of his writings, Ellis commented that strong, resistant irrational beliefs must be met with forceful disputing, first by the therapist and then in conjunction with the client. Exaggerated activating events are put into perspective when we dispute them with another person. A significant amount of REBT sessions are dedicated to actively disputing what Ellis called 'insane' or irrational thoughts. An example of a personal homework sheet that employs the ABC model (plus disputing) can be seen in Table 4.1.

E - Effective new philosophy

Clients are encouraged to apply the rational practice of REBT in the real world. The therapist will often ask clients to engage in homework which applies the ABC model (initially to stressful situations). The client subsequently disputes these irrational beliefs on paper and with time and practice, acquires a new effective REBT philosophy which can be employed without the therapists help. Albert Ellis viewed the REBT therapist as an educator who would encourage the client to practice observing and disputing irrational beliefs, first in the presence of the counsellor and secondly as homework to be discussed at subsequent sessions. The end goal is to create a self-reliant client who no longer requires the expertise of a psychotherapist.

REBT and phobias - facing your fears

When Ellis was 19 he decided to take heed of advice he read in a philosophy book and face his fear head on. One of his phobias at the time was that of approaching women of his own age. Ellis set himself the task of approaching as many women as he could in the Bronx Botanical Garden (New York). He reasoned with himself that dying was the worst thing that could happen! He eventually approached 130 women and didn't die! You can read Ellis's account of his adventures in the Bronx Botanical garden online (www.rebtnetwork.org). This desensitisation or over exposure to fear, worked for Ellis and he subsequently incorporated it into his developing theories on treating emotional disturbance. This counterintuitive approach to resolving personal fears is similar to the paradoxical intention, first formulated by Viktor Frankl (Chapter Three).

Brief therapy

Albert Ellis contended that REBT is potentially the briefest form of therapy, even when compared with other cognitive schools. He believed clients could be exposed to the ABC(DE) method quickly, often in the first session. Positive results can subsequently emerge rapidly with the proviso that the client works hard both inside and outside of the counselling room.

Ellis and Gloria

You might remember me describing (Chapter Five) a much viewed video experiment, which was filmed in the 1960s to showcase the up and coming psychotherapies of the day. Carl Rogers, Fritz Perls and Albert Ellis were asked to provide examples of their new types of therapy using the same client, Gloria (a young American mother). I remember the first time I saw this video vividly. It filled me with admiration for Carl Rogers and his elegant, gentle style which seemed to endear Gloria to him. Conversely, the actions of both Fritz Perls and Albert Ellis shocked me. They came across as rude, confrontational and aggressive; the complete antithesis to what I thought counselling was supposed to be about. With the advent of YouTube, these sentiments have become shared by thousands of student counsellors around the world.

Stephen Weinrach (a disciple of Ellis and REBT), has lamented the fact that this video has tainted Ellis and his theories. In fact, Ellis himself supposedly regretted the session. Weinrach has criticised counselling schools for perpetuating misconceptions about REBT by showing this video and deterring future psychotherapists from studying REBT. To be fair, this video is readily available on YouTube and it wouldn't matter if colleges struck it from their syllabi or not. However, Weinrach is right by suggesting that we shouldn't let this single example deter the study of REBT as an effective, efficient form of therapy.

Date	A Activating Event	B Beliefs	C Consequence	D Dispute
2010	Received an invite to a colleagues' house warming party.	Nobody will talk to me. Everyone will make fun of me in work for being a loner who doesn't know how to socialise. I'm a loser.	I declined the invitation. My colleague was upset with me. I felt bad, which confirmed my belief that I'm a loser.	What is the worst that could have happened if you attended? Many people feel anxious about social get-togethers. Does that make you a loser? The next time, could you bring a friend and plan to introduce yourself to one person there (as a start)? What if the person you introduce yourself to does speak with you? Will that dispel your belief about nobody talking with you? Could you plan to stay for a fixed time and then make polite goodbye? How will you plan for your next invite?

Table 4.1 Example of a homework sheet that makes use of the Reality Therapy ABC model.

Aaron Beck's Cognitive therapy

Aaron Beck (born in 1921) is an American psychiatrist who along with Carl Rogers and Albert Ellis was one of the most influential psychotherapists of the 20th century. In 1954, after some years as an army psychiatrist, Beck took up a position at the University of Pennsylvania Medical School. From this point onward he became slowly disillusioned with the psychoanalytic approach; psychoanalysis simply wasn't working with many of his patients. Research into the dreams of depressed patients led him to the conclusion that in many cases it was the patient's cognition (thoughts) that lay at the heart of depression. A very pragmatic and efficient man, Beck developed a number of meticulous theories that went on to form the basis of Cognitive therapy. In short, people develop core beliefs and assumptions based upon early life experiences. These core beliefs are triggered by events or other people, which in turn lead to distorted thoughts, which cause disturbing emotions. Disturbing emotions lead to disrupted behaviour, which brings us to a new event that triggers the cycle again. Beck and his theories have spawned a number of protégés, who are now world leaders in their own right, not least his daughter Judith Beck. Judith Beck among others refined her father's theories into practical, easy to follow formulations (Figure 6.2) that have been tailored specifically for depression, anxiety, panic, post-traumatic stress disorder (PTSD), eating disorders, obsessive compulsive disorder (OCD) and substance abuse.

These formulations can now be found in the office of almost every Cognitive behavioural therapist in the world. Their simplicity and clarity is regarded as their strength; theoretically it allows each Cognitive therapist to provide the same therapy the world over. This universal application means that Beck's Cognitive therapy can be researched easily: the formulations and their associated questionnaires (or inventories) and homework assignments can be easily compared across hundreds of clients from different clinics, all over the world. Consequently, Cognitive therapy in particular is the most studied psychotherapy in the world and universally adopted by the medical system. At last, doctors had a psychotherapy that could be empirically evaluated in terms of diagnosis and patient outcome.

The nuts and bolts of cognitive formulations

Early experience

Although Cognitive therapy (like Choice theory and REBT) is focused primarily on the present, it does recognise that many behavioural and cognitive problems have their origin in past early experiences.

Cognitive Schemas and core beliefs

Cognitive schemas[2] are probably the closest you can get in CBT to the *unconscious* described in psychoanalysis. They are regarded as the highest order of thought that can lie partially unconscious and consist of a number of basic beliefs and assumptions all based on the same theme, such as a harsh and unloving parent. These core beliefs (for example: *I believe that I am unlovable*) form the basis of all subsequent thoughts, which are related to specific schemas and are crucial to Cognitive therapy and alleviating the client's symptoms.

Assumptions

All assumptions can be defined in terms of 'If.......then......' statements.

"**If** I go to the party **then** nobody will talk to me."

Assumptions come directly from embedded core beliefs and lead to negative automatic thoughts and some form of action.

Negative automatic thoughts (NATs)

Whenever any counselling student hears or reads the acronym NAT they are immediately drawn to Cognitive Therapy and CBT. We all have them. They are persistently there and seem to flow from some perpetual inexhaustible source. Just like any waterfall, the constant flow of NATs will eventually erode the rock below. Some of the many examples of NATs include:

"I'm a bloody Idiot."
"Why do I always do that?"
"That's bloody typical of me."
"I'm doomed to fail."
"Other people succeed but not me."
"I'm ugly."
"I'm fat."
"I can't do this."
"I'm a loser."

Certain events or people attract their corresponding and appropriate NATs in our brain. These events are called triggers.

---

[2] Schema therapy is obviously based on this concept and will be described in more detail at the end of this chapter.

Triggers

Taking the example above, we could probably guess that the following NATs might be associated with the trigger of being invited to a dinner party:

"I'm ugly."
"I'm fat."
"I can't do this."
"I'm a loser."

While the trigger of being rejected in an interview might be associated with the following:

"I'm an Idiot."
"That's typical of me."
"I'm doomed to fail."
"Other people succeed but not me."
"I'm a loser."

Beck believed that by changing our clinging to specific NATs, suffering clients could eventually alter their core beliefs and generate new, more positive schemas. So we can see that although we all seem to have a constant stream of NATs, only certain NATs become attached to specific triggers. NATs which associate with particular triggers frequently evoke powerful negative emotion.

Emotion

All sorts of emotions might emerge for the two examples given above. It's easy to imagine feeling *anxious* and *panicked* about the thought of a dinner party, if you believed that you were socially inadequate. Likewise with failing an interview, you might be simultaneously *sad* and *angry* with yourself, should you believe deep down that you are incompetent and doomed to fail. Such powerful emotions almost always lead to a reaction in the form of physical behaviour.

Behaviour

The type of behaviours manifesting from all the myriad of emotions any person might have are obviously infinite, so we will confine ourselves to the examples given above. If I believe that I am socially inadequate then I will become anxious about a dinner invitation. Nobody likes feeling anxious so *I will decide not to go to the party*. If I believe that I am inherently incompetent then when I don't get the job I'll become angry with myself and despondent. I might subsequently decide not to go for any more interviews and stay in a job that depresses me.

Consequences

Like all others, the actions or behaviours described in the previous section will have consequences, unforeseen or not. Unfortunately, such consequences tend to re-enforce core beliefs, assumptions and NATs and the cycle begins again. For example, my friend might not invite me to anymore get-togethers, thus compounding my belief that I am socially incompetent. By not applying for any more jobs or lacking interest in work, my peers might be promoted above me, thereby 'proving' that I am incompetent. These core beliefs link to more NATs, more negative emotion and so on *ad infinitum*.

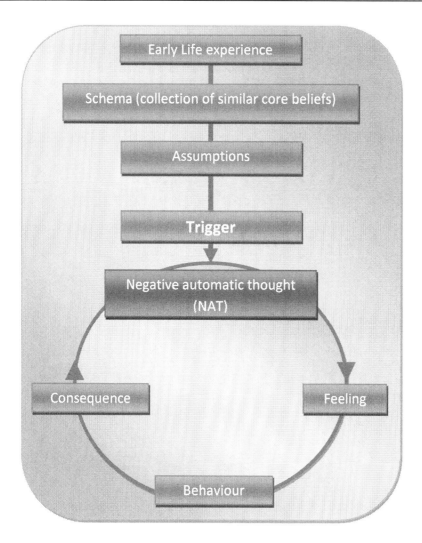

Figure 4.2 Judith Beck's longitudinal formulation of cognition.

Specific formulations for different problems

The Cognitive therapist, Frank Wills has compiled a table that summarises the different themes associated with different mental health issues (Table 4.2). Many researchers have noticed that some individuals suffering from specific ailments tend to share similar underlying themes. These themes come from similar schemas/core beliefs and lead to similar assumptions and NATs.

Problem	Cognitive Theme
Depression	Loss, defeat
Anxiety	Danger, threat
Panic	Physical, mental catastrophe
OCD	Inflated responsibility
Substance abuse	Permissive belief
Eating disorders	Self-criticism
Social anxiety	Fear of evaluation
PTSD	Impending threat

Table 4.2. Different mental health issues are often associated with specific cognitive themes that can be inputted into specific formulations (adapted from Beck's Cognitive Therapy by Frank Wills).

Judith Beck's core principles of Cognitive Therapy

In a book she co-wrote with her father, *Cognitive Therapy: basics and beyond* (1995), Judith Beck provided 11 principles, which she believed were the cornerstones of Cognitive therapy. These include:

1. Cognitive Therapy is based on the perpetually evolving formulation of the client and his or her problem. In other words, the counsellor must constantly revise formulations and treatment plans in collaboration with the client; Cognitive therapy is a dynamic process.

2. The therapeutic relationship between client and counsellor is crucial to a successful outcome.

3. Collaboration and participation are crucial to a successful outcome.

4. Time limited. Cognitive Therapy is brief therapy, normally lasting between 10 and 20 sessions.

5. Counselling sessions are structured and directed by the therapist.

6. Cognitive therapy is goal oriented.

7. There is a strong emphasis on the here and now.

8. Cognitive therapists engage in psycho-education so that clients can help themselves and become self-sufficient.

9. Engaging in homework tasks is essential to a successful outcome.

10. Cognitive therapists help the client identify, evaluate and respond to dysfunctional thoughts.

11. Cognitive therapy uses a variety of techniques designed to alter feelings, thoughts and behaviour.

The practice of Cognitive Therapy

I will provide a brief example of a formulation devised for depression and where the Cognitive therapist might intervene. In cases such as these, the counsellor must try to intervene at all junctures of the formulation which includes: schemas/core beliefs, assumptions, NATs, feelings, behaviours and consequences (Figure 4.3.).

You can see from Figure 4.3 that Cognitive therapists must get a picture of the client's background and back-story in order to devise a suitable and individual formulation. As previously mentioned, Cognitive counsellors don't dwell on the past. Assumptions ('if.....then....' statements) can be challenged by the counsellor during the session; the client can practice this at home. In particular, the logic and validity of the assumptions are tested. If a client assumes that he will die upon entering a busy shopping centre, the counsellor will test the veracity of this statement.

Thought records are very useful in highlighting the client's NATs, which can in many cases be semi-unconscious. The client is urged to pay more attention to his thoughts and note any negative ones. He or she subsequently writes down the facts that both support and reject these thoughts. If the thought is negative, the client must write a more realistic alternative. The entry can be concluded by the client rating his depression out of 10. This can help the client realise how NATs are often associated with more severe bouts of depression. Thought records are invaluable to Cognitive therapy and have proved essential aids in helping the therapist re-educate the client and prevent future relapse. A huge number of CBT homework sheets that include thought records, can be seen and/or downloaded from www.psychologytools.org.

Relaxation techniques are very useful tools in arresting strong emotion that can so often have severe physiological effects such as profuse sweating, shaking, fainting and increased heart rate. Simple abdominal breathing (breathing from the tummy) instead of the chest, for just 60 seconds can have an amazing impact on strong emotions and limit their effects on the body. More prolonged meditation techniques can also be applied. Mindfulness, which will be discussed later in this chapter, is also very good for disengaging with NATs and defusing strong emotions as they begin. In short, mindfulness means just that, being mindful of each and every action and thought for a period of 10 minutes or so. Clients are encouraged to accept whatever thoughts and emotions that arise. Practicing mindfulness serves to calm the mind and body.

Behavioural intervention is another stalwart of Cognitive Therapy that can require a great deal of trust on the client's behalf. In the case described in Figure 4.3., the therapist might suggest a small behavioural experiment whereby client and counsellor go out for a coffee in a nearby cafe. After gradual exposure to busy public spaces the therapist might set the client the task of merely introducing him or herself to a stranger at an appropriate event such as an art exhibition. In these experiments Cognitive therapists are present and on standby should the client feel overwhelmed. The client is urged to keep records of their thoughts on the experiment; they grade their depression out of 10 before and after the event. In addition, they take note of their anxious thoughts and assumptions prior to the experiment and whether or not these thoughts were validated afterwards.

Importantly, Cognitive therapists review the client's progress after each set of experiments and homework assignments. Frequent alterations in the formulation are essential to a successful outcome.

In subsequent sessions, Cognitive therapists will engage in a routine check list that includes:

- Mood check – how is the client feeling; how would she or he grade their emotion out of 10.

- Attend to any immediate symptoms, such as panic by perhaps engaging in relaxation techniques.

- Assess long term goals (long term in Cognitive therapy is normal between 10 and 20 sessions, maximum).

- Set the session agenda.

- Review and provide feedback on homework assignments.

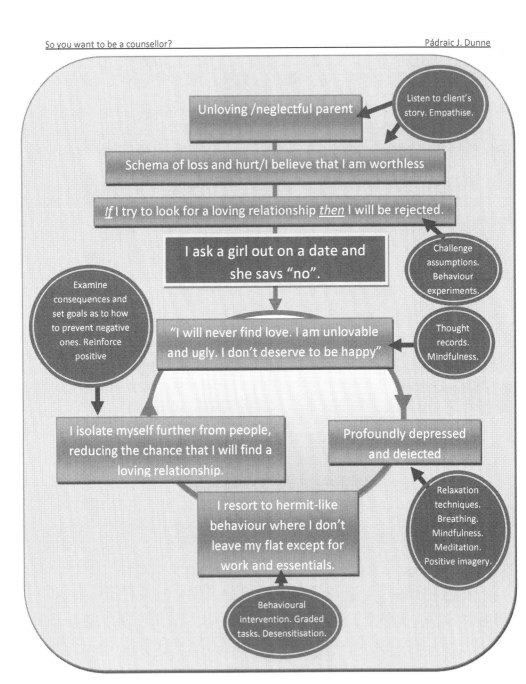

Figure 4.3. Therapeutical intervention (purple circles) in a case of depression, using Judith Beck's longitudinal formulation guide.

The third wave of CBT

Steven Hayes lists the following emerging modalities as being part of the third wave of CBT: Acceptance and Commitment therapy (ACT), Dialectical Behaviour Therapy, Functional Analytic Psychotherapy, Integrative Behavioural Couples Therapy (IBCT), Mindfulness-Based Cognitive Therapy (MBCT) and Schema Therapy. Academics and researchers have struggled to come up with any singular unifying concept among the different third wave modalities. However, these emerging therapies seem to be less didactic (designed to teach or educate) and more experiential when compared with Cognitive therapy. Furthermore, they appear to strongly emphasise context, i.e. the space the client resides in rather than mechanism, such as case formulations and thought record sheets.

ACT

It is suggested by the pioneers of ACT, such as Stephen Hayes and Russ Harris that the most significant cause of unhappiness in western societies today is this flawed and incorrect view that happiness is the default state for all humans. Any human who deviates from this apparent norm is subsequently deemed to be abnormal. ACT practitioners profoundly disagree with this point of view and posit rather that the contrary is true: unhappiness, suffering, pain, anxiety and depression are in fact part of what it means to be a normal human being. By accepting these universal truths we can move one step closer to living in the reality of the present, where suffering exists but does not necessarily have to control us as individuals. For Steven Hayes, ACT represents a holistic approach, based on examining the entire context in which thoughts feelings and behaviour arise and does not examine cognition in isolation, like CBT. The key process that ACT (Figure 4.4) seeks to promote in each client is flexibility.

The core processes of ACT

Acceptance
Acceptance is used in an attempt to counter avoidance. Clients are encouraged to feel anxiety as a feeling as well as to feel pain itself; this not as a passive resignation to suffering but rather an active willingness to include the negative.

Cognitive defusion

Fusing with thoughts reduces our capacity for flexibility. Unlike CBT, ACT practitioners don't seek to alter negative thoughts, merely the behavioural response to the thought. There is some empirical evidence showing that **word repetition** (saying the problematic word or phrase out loud repeatedly until it loses meaning) is one of the most effective ways to combat cognitive fusion (Masuda, A., 2004. Cognitive defusion and self-relevant negative thoughts: examining the impact of a ninety year old technique. *Behaviour Research and Therapy, 42*(4), 477-485). Applying external attributes to negative thoughts also works. Troublesome thoughts can be given dimensions, colour or smell so that they transform from insidious external things to less threatening external objects.

Being present

Being present involves a non-judgemental constant examination of the present moment in terms of thoughts, emotion and experience. Mindfulness exercises have been proven to help here.

Self as context

Sometimes we get stuck in a certain role based on the labels and descriptions we have for ourselves; such labels come from our past and significant others in our lives as well as society at large and even the media. A rigid idea of who we are (a stupid boy; a broken girl, the responsible eldest) can help foment a very inflexible psychological frame of mind. Furthermore, by labelling yourself as depressed or anxious, you restrict yourself to that label. The goal here is not to generate new labels but instead to recognise that we possess minds that label constantly.

Values

Values are abstract aspirations that add meaning to life. Usually the client collaborates with the ACT therapist to generate a plan of action as to how to attain or aspire to these values. This is part of the commitment stage of ACT.

Committed action

ACT treatment regimens almost always involve work linked with helping clients achieve their goals (that remain linked to the values described above). Committed actions help counter avoidance, impulsivity and passive coping styles.

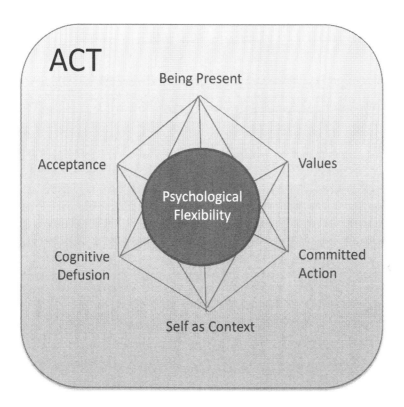

Figure 4.4. Adapted from: Steven Hayes, et al (2013). Acceptance and Commitment Therapy and Contextual Behavioral Science: Examining the Progress of a Distinctive Model of Behavioral and Cognitive Therapy. *Behavior Therapy, 44*(2), 180-198.

Schema therapy

Schema therapy was developed by the American psychologist Jeffrey E. Young who realised that Cognitive therapy didn't work in all situations, particularly for clients diagnosed with Borderline Personality Disorder (BPD)[3].

As we have seen in the previous section on Cognitive therapy, schemas represent high order thoughts and beliefs that tend to be associated around a central theme. Similar schemas are formed in cases of extreme neglect, where the child's basic emotional and physical needs are not met. Like psychodynamic theory, Schema therapy often focuses on childhood memories and how they might have impacted on the client. Furthermore, Schema therapy has borrowed from other CBT traditions in terms of practicality and developed 18 common schemas that can be ordered under 5 distinct 'Domains'. These domains and their associated schemas can be seen in Table 4.3.

Essentials of Schema therapy

The therapeutic relationship

Schema Questionnaire (www.schematherapy.com/id49.htm)

Experimentation - Schema therapists often ask clients to engage in empty chair exercises where they can figuratively speak with significant others of their past and present. In addition, clients are frequently asked to give further voice to long-since pent-up emotion by writing to those responsible for their maladaptive schemas. Other exercises include asking the client to speak as if he or she was back in a traumatic childhood moment and to speak as the child might. Based upon a strong therapeutic alliance, these activities can have a transformative effect on clients.

Forgiveness - This remains one of the final steps of the process; the client must forgive him or herself as well as those who have hurt them. The goal of Schema therapy is to ultimately weaken entrenched schemas, promote healing through open discussion in conjunction with the exercises described above and provide clients with coping strategies in future times of crisis.

---

[3] The essential feature of Borderline Personality Disorder is a pervasive pattern of instability of interpersonal relationships, self-image, and affects, and marked impulsivity that begins by early adulthood and is present in a variety of contexts. Individuals with Borderline Personality Disorder make frantic efforts to avoid real or imagined abandonment (taken from the DSM-IV-TR (2004) Criteria for Diagnosis of Borderline Personality Disorder).

Schemas and Modes

As described, Schema theory in particular has been used to treat those with BPD. Unlike other established disorders, which can be interminably rigid, such as OCD, clients with BPD can be dynamic and explosive. The client's needs, wants and emotions are volatile and can change from session to session. To cope with this type of fluid disorder, Young devised the term mode. Modes may be described as a group of active Schemas. Early adaptive schemas and their domains can be seen in Table 4.3.

Domains				
Disconnection & Rejection	**Impaired Autonomy**	**Impaired Limits**	**Other Directedness**	**Over-vigilance & Inhibition**
Modes and their Schemas				
Abandonment	Dependence & Incompetence	Entitlement & Grandiosity	Subjugation	Negativity & Pessimism
Mistrust/abuse	Vulnerability to harm or illness	Insufficient self-control/self-discipline	Self-sacrifice	Emotional inhibition
Emotional deprivation	Enmeshment or undeveloped self			Unrelenting standards & hyper criticalness
Defectiveness & Shame	Failure			Punitiveness
Social isolation				

Table 4.3. Early maladaptive schemas and their domains.

Mindfulness

The concept of mindfulness is as old as Buddhism itself, which originated in India approximately 2500 years ago. It is used by Buddhists around the world to help bring a concentrated focus on the present moment as well as bringing awareness to the mind and body. In the 1980s, Jon Kabat Zinn, a doctor and avid meditator began to apply a type of mindfulness developed by Vietnamese monk Thích Nhất Hạnh, to patients in his clinic in the US. Zinn experimented with a mindfulness program (Mindfulness-based stress reduction; MBSR) that was eventually extended to 8 weeks and would incorporate mindfulness meditation with basic yoga. Initially applied to terminally ill patients who suffered a great deal of pain and death anxiety, mindfulness was subsequently used to treat chronic pain, depression, anxiety and other illnesses. As a treatment, it has become profoundly successful.

Since its inception in the 1980s as a tool of western psychotherapy, mindfulness has spread round the world and even become incorporated into CBT. MBSR programs are taught in many colleges and universities, one of the most prominent being the Centre for Mindfulness Research and Practice at Bangor University, Wales.

What is meditation?

For some, meditation represents an esoteric religious ritual, practiced only by Tibetan monks. The truth is that meditation is for everybody. Taken in its simplest form, mediation is paying attention to the breath. When we start to pay attention to the cyclic inhalation and exhalation of our breath, we find that our mind begins to calm and slow down. Our thoughts don't shut down altogether; the meditator merely becomes less attached to them.

More advanced meditation involves a thorough examination of the multitude of thoughts that seem to arise in our minds, second by second. This type of meditation can help identify the negative automatic thoughts and help the mediator understand how his or her mind operates at any given time. This type of meditation also helps us realise that we are not our thoughts. It becomes clear that our thoughts arise all by themselves, independent of awareness or will. If that is the case then negative automatic thoughts are not really part of our purposeful awareness at all. In other words, if thoughts emerge independently and randomly from our brain, then we don't have to necessarily put so much credence in them.

Studies have shown that regular meditation (30 minutes per day) can alter the physiology of the brain. Functional magnetic resonance imaging (fMRI) scanning technologies have allowed researchers to examine the various pertinent areas of the brain during meditation. These investigators have found that areas associated with reason (the pre-frontal cortex situated at the front of the brain) become thicker and more capable of controlling the emotional centre, located in the amygdala (a relatively small area found near the central bottom part of the brain). Additional studies have shown that regular meditation lowers blood pressure, helps regulate blood glucose levels and promotes a healthy immune system. These reports are produced by reputable research groups from prestigious institutions, such as Harvard University and published in high impact medical and science journals.

The MBSR program as devised by Jon Kabat Zinn

Although Jon Kabat Zinn wasn't the first westerner to integrate mindfulness with modern medicine and psychotherapy, he is probably the most renowned practitioner among medical/psychotherapy circles; the fact that he is a medical doctor has helped those in the wider medical community take heed of its potential. Zinn's mindfulness program (as well as many others around the world) is broken into 8 weeks. As the weeks progress, the practices become longer and more varied until eventually the participant is ready to practice mindfulness without the support of teachers or fellow participants. When Zinn first organised these programs in the 1980s, they were held predominantly in hospitals with very sick people as the participants. These days you can probably find a mindfulness course in every major city.

Mindfulness programs can be difficult, particularly if you've never meditated before. It's especially hard to begin something new if you are in pain, depressed or extremely anxious. Regardless, Zinn stresses to prospective participants and his patients that "You don't have to like it; you just have to do it." He and other teachers in the field also emphasise that you should really practice every day, if you want to reap the full rewards of mindfulness. Weekly group meetings help participants keep on track and provide much needed support. I am not going to go into all the details of a mindfulness based program. Instead I would like to simply highlight some of the essential components.

Breathing

All meditation starts with the breath. Sounds simple doesn't it? We do it without thinking right? Do you breathe from your chest or your belly? Do you breathe fully at any stage during the day (really emptying your lungs)? Very few of us do this and normally confine our breathing to shallow chest breathing. As well as having positive physiological effects, deep breathing helps focus the mind away from distracting thoughts.

Participants of mindfulness based stress reduction programs are encouraged to take at least 10 minutes every day to engage in deep abdominal breathing. The idea is to cultivate awareness about how your mind reacts to various internal and external stimuli. Often when we are anxious, depressed or in pain we focus inward, usually increasing the emotions or pain that we are trying to avoid. By enhancing awareness of our body, mind and the environment around us, we can alleviate much of the intensity of these powerful emotions and sensations. Anxiety and depression usually emanate from preoccupation with past events or worries about the future; by training our brains to remain for the most part in the present, we can help stave off this type of mental suffering.

The body scan

Much of the first few weeks of the program involve listening to guided meditations, the most common being the body scan. Briefly, participants are asked to scan slowly through their whole body, starting with the toes of the left foot and ending with the face. You will be invited to breathe deeply into these parts of your body. Once you have finishing scanning your body, you are subsequently invited to rest in what hopefully is a calm state and monitor your thoughts as well as any sensations emerging from your body. The whole process normally takes 30 minutes.

Those pesky thoughts

Thoughts can really mess up your tranquil meditation! In mindfulness, the goal is to acknowledge all of your thoughts, good and bad. You must try not to react to these thoughts and become carried away with them. One common mistake is to try and forcefully eject negative thoughts or disturbing memories from awareness. All thoughts must be accepted and put behind you. By constantly coming back to present awareness we practice staying in the moment and strengthen our capacity to withstand negative and overwhelming emotion. In essence, mindfulness is akin to a gym for the mind.

Yoga

Yoga is a big part of the mindfulness program but don't be deterred by that. The selection of postures required in the mindfulness program are not very difficult; you're not expected to wrap one leg around your head while standing on the other. However, if you do have back or joint issues, do check with your doctor before you proceed. In short, yoga is a type of physical meditation where you bring awareness to your body. It is the perfect preparation for meditation, because at the end you feel energised but very calm. See Jon Kabat Zinn's book for descriptions and illustrations of the yoga postures applied during mindfulness programs. For more details on this program including the various yoga postures, please see Zinn's very accessible book, "Full Catastrophe Living".

Acceptance

As humans, we often want to obliterate negative thoughts and emotion. We escape strong emotions and negative memories through sex, drugs including alcohol, or relentless entertainment through TV, computer games as well as gambling in all its guises. Others escape through work and career. We don't want to face the shadow within and in extreme cases we can go to extreme lengths to suppress these dark aspects of ourselves. Accepting our thoughts and emotions as they randomly swim across our mind or bubble up from the depths, can be the start of accepting our shadow side and any heretofore hidden traumas.

Mindfulness-based Cognitive Therapy (MBCT)

MBCT has been pioneered by Segal, Williams and Teadale in the 1990s and is based on work by Jon Jabat Zinn on Mindfulness. Segal and colleagues modified Zinn's program to incorporate elements of Cognitive therapy into an 8 week program. The result is an intriguing combination of cognitive therapy, relaxation techniques in conjunction with the core elements of ACT. The goal is to encourage clients to disengage from disruptive thoughts and focus on the present by being mindful of internal and external processes. Like ACT, MBCT encourages engagement with difficult emotions and experiences to combat avoidance (Crane, 2009).

A lot of small research studies have tested the efficacy in a very wide range of conditions from depression to blood pressure. Although effective, more in depth studies with larger sample bases are required for this fledgling modality. Nevertheless, MBCT does compare well with Cognitive therapy, especially where relapse rates from depression are concerned.

Summary

- Choice theory posits that mental issues arise when one or more of our basic needs are not met. Such issues are intrinsically linked to our relationships with other human beings. As a result, people choose to be depressed or anxious. Reality therapy encourages clients to take responsibility for that which is in their control and instead to choose not to be depressed or anxious. Together with the therapist, clients plan to achieve their ideal quality world.

- REBT is a practical therapy focused on the present and suggests that emotional disturbances occur when we falsely interpret the world around us. Like Choice theory, REBT encourages clients to take responsibility for their behaviour and actively choose not to suffer.

- Cognitive therapy is a practical psychotherapy that requires collaboration between client and therapist. Its' primary focus is psycho-education, enabling clients to acquire the tools to help themselves. It is based on the theory that people develop core beliefs and assumptions based upon early life experiences. These core beliefs are triggered by events or other people, which in turn lead to distorted thoughts, which cause disturbing emotions.

- The first wave of CBT was represented by behavioural theories and research carried out in the mid-20th century by psychologists such as B.F. Skinner. Choice theory, REBT and Cognitive therapy are regarded as the second wave of CBT, while the recent third wave is said to comprise modalities such as ACT, Schema therapy and MBCT among others.

- The primary goal of ACT is to help clients establish a more flexible self. This involves accepting and residing in the present moment and changing behaviour that leads to a meaningful life.

- Schema therapy is an extension of Cognitive therapy that employs experiential tools similar to those used in Gestalt therapy (such as the empty chair technique). It is focused on helping clients to identify early maladaptive schemas or core beliefs caused early trauma. Schema therapists work with a number of different modes (groups of schemas) that are active within the client at any given time.

- MBSR and MBCT are programs based on mindfulness meditation, the primary focus of which is to learn acceptance of thoughts and emotions. A by-product of mindfulness meditation is stress reduction.

Reading list

- Choice Theory: A New Psychology of Personal Freedom by William Glasser
- Rational emotive behaviour therapy: a reader by Windy Dryden
- Cognitive Behavior Therapy: Basics and Beyond by Aaron T. Beck and Judith S. Beck
- Feeling Good: The New Mood Therapy by David D. Burns
- Schema Therapy: Distinctive Features (CBT Distinctive Features) by Eshkol Rafaeli, David P. Bernstein and Jeffrey Young
- Full Catastrophe Living by Jon Kabat Zinn
- Buddha's Brain: The Practical Neuroscience of Happiness, Love, and Wisdom by Rick Hanson and Richard Mendius

Section Two:
Studying Counselling

Chapter Five

Personal Development

I can't emphasise enough how important personal development is for me and for all emerging counsellors. We owe it to ourselves and our clients to air out each and every dusty nook and cranny of our minds (as much as we're able to anyway). Dismissing personal development assumes perfection and renders the counsellor blind to any unforeseen minefields that will inevitably arise in the counselling room. At least if you are aware of the minefield you can make the appropriate precautions to protect you and your client. There seems to be no hard and fast protocol for personal development, only that it is ongoing and should last for at least as long as you plan to remain a counsellor. That might seem dramatic but anything less in my view can only lead to trouble. It doesn't mean that a counsellor must always be 'on', just that we should strive to take ourselves out of our comfort zones every now and again. If we do this I think we can avoid the day when we believe we know what's best for our clients and how to fix them; as counsellors, we can't fix anybody. When those thoughts enter your head, it's time for the women and children to head screaming for the life boats.

Get the counsellor you deserve – one that makes you work!

This is a very important decision. Your counsellor will be instrumental in your development as a person throughout your student years. You should take a number of things under consideration before you make this decision:

- **Is your counsellor accredited by a governing body such as the European Association for Counselling?** Accreditation is a requirement for most colleges and universities. When looking for my counsellor I called no less than seven people in the Dublin area, only five of which were accredited but all of them were charging a similar fee!

- This leads me nicely to my second point, **money**. Always try and appeal to the inner student in any counsellor you call. Ask them for a student discount.

- **You need to like your counsellor**. My counsellor was recommended to me by a tutor and his style of counselling (predominantly person-centred) was exactly what I needed at the time. What if you don't like your counsellor? Well it could be that he or she is challenging you and you're resisting this challenge because it's a personal sore spot. If that's the case then you might need to give your counsellor more time to help you get to the bottom of this resistance. On the other hand, you might simply not like your counsellor, in which case, move! Counselling can be expensive and you don't want to waste your time or the counsellors' by staying longer than you should. Your counsellor might be a lovely person but the particular school of counselling he or she comes from might not be what you need at the time. However, if you're finding that you have visited seven counsellors in a row and none of them appealed, the problem might reside with you and less with the counsellor.

- **Try different types of counselling**. Over the course of your personal therapy you might like to get experience of different types of counselling. Sometimes, different counselling modes can help with different types of issues.

  For example, I realised that I was becoming obsessive about checking whether my car was locked or not. I would drive to the train station in the morning, park the car, lock it, and walk to the platform only to have to return to the car to check that it was locked. I missed my train a number of times because of this behaviour and not once had I returned to find an unlocked car. Clearly, I was developing some issue here. I eventually faced this behaviour with a two pronged approach that included standard Person Centred Therapy with Cognitive Behavioural Therapy (CBT). CBT helped me stop this compulsive checking with the use of thought records and basic good mental housekeeping. Each time I closed and locked the car, I would write in my notebook, "car locked and checked" with the date and time. Eventually I managed to alter my behaviour, although I still fall back into similar behaviour when I'm under stress. If I do, then I simply pull out my notebook and begin recording my activity once again. Importantly for me, I was able to get to the root of this compulsive behaviour with the help of my counsellor. I am occasionally prone to bouts of low self esteem and haven't always had a great deal of confidence in myself. As a result I can be hyper sensitive to any form of criticism no matter how mild. It is surprising how relieving it is to examine your past and the potential sources of your current behaviour. It provides perspective and allows you to foster compassion for yourself as a small child. I believe it's also important to look at the other people involved and if possible, forgive them their role in the matter. I am not going to go into the details of my childhood, in order to protect the people involved. It wasn't terribly traumatic, I wasn't abused but I did develop a sense of inferiority, which ultimately (I believe) led me to develop some minor compulsive behaviour such as checking whether or not my car was locked.

  I should stress that the example I just gave is of a very minor compulsion. I am in no way making light of those with serious obsessive compulsive behaviour, who suffer greatly and require a lot of help from trained counsellors. I am merely trying to provide a real example of how different types of counselling can help solve different problems in the same person. So what does this mean for me as a counsellor? Well, for one, I have to be very careful not to respond when a client criticises me. It has happened already and although I felt the old urges to respond by hiding in my shell, I forced myself to maintain a professional demeanour. The client deserves nothing less. It is getting easier to take criticism but I must always be wary of it interfering with my work as a counsellor.

Some extra considerations

My course stipulates a minimum of 50 hours personal therapy prior to receipt of a diploma and/or degree in counselling. This is in line with one of the Irish governing bodies (Irish Association for Counselling and Psychotherapy; IACP). What if you have no burning issue, do you still have to do 50 hours? The short answer is yes. Some people have issues with this. It has been argued that students of counselling and psychotherapy will be at various stages of personal development: some need at least 50 hours while others require considerably less. Maybe there should be an allowance for those with no immediate need to see counsellors, who have a significant of hours under their belt? I have found that the last fifteen sessions or so with my counsellor turned into a type of cosy chat about counselling in general. This was great. As I said, I like my counsellor and I'm always eager to learn from experienced counsellors but this wasn't therapy anymore. It doesn't mean that I won't need counselling in the future; thankfully for now I don't feel the need. Regardless of all the debate, most students will have to attend a counsellor for a significant number of hours as part of their training. You can't expect a client to sit in that chair if you've never sat in it yourself.

The value of keeping a journal

This may seem an alien concept to you but I promise that if you start a journal, it will become one of the most helpful things you could do, on a personal and professional level. I keep two types of journals but I'm sure you could get away with one.

As students, we were advised to maintain a personal journal from the foundation course onward. I resisted this at first (I'm not sure why); I think I had the idea that journaling was one step above a teenager's angst ridden diary and just didn't see the point. Nevertheless, I bought myself a nice new Moleskine notebook and started to record daily entries. Once I got over the feeling that I had to write as if someone was going to read it, things started to flow. I started to honestly record my thoughts and feelings, no matter how dark, flippant or unpleasant. It helped me to move into a position where I was actively monitoring my thoughts and emotions in real time. That probably sounds exhausting but it's quite the opposite. You tend to focus on the present more, which leaves less room for anxieties from the past or future to nestle in your head. Of course, like all good practices for me, they can fall by the wayside when things start going badly, which is something I have to be vigilant about.

Journaling helps you forensically examine your fleeting thoughts and emotions and can help identify areas that need work. Unfortunately, it probably won't help you locate your blind spots (only a counsellor can do that) but it will accelerate personal development. Practically speaking, it will also be an enormous source of material for any personal-based essays you have to write for your course.

Little black book

I often carry a little notebook in my pocket and take it with me everywhere. It wasn't just for personal development. I recorded all sorts of ideas and lists of things to do in it as well as the occasional thought record (mentioned in the previous section). A little notebook will help you gather those killer essay titles that pop into your head while waiting for a bus or in line at the checkout. By opening your brain to the possibility of catching fleeting thoughts, you will be surprised by the amount of good ideas that pop into your head and in the strangest of places. It is also very useful to record any topics (including dreams) you might like to discuss with your counsellor. Lately, I have replaced my little notebook with my phone. Either way, I find it a very useful accessory for college and life in general. I think you might too.

The use of art in personal development

This may not seem an obvious route to personal development but it can be a fun way to examine your mental processes. You don't have to be Van Gogh or Michael Angelo; stick figures and plasticine are good enough. Try and stay clear of wanting to make your art perfect. Ignore those negative voices that tell you "You're no good at art, what are you doing?" It's not about entering an art competition, it's about personal development and doing something you enjoy in the process. I was first asked to draw some pictures in a counselling setting by the first counsellor I attended in my late 20s. I hadn't drawn or painted anything in years; it seemed a bit weird for a grown man to be using colouring pencils. Once I started I couldn't stop. I drew picture after picture and loved every minute of it. I wasn't sure how it contributed to my counselling and they weren't masterpieces by any means but I was glad that I started something that I really loved to do as a kid. My counsellor at the time gave me some suggestions as to what they might mean and suggested a common thread. It was fun and I haven't stopped drawing since, in fact I've moved on to painting pictures with my daughter, which I enjoy more than most things. Give it a go; if nothing else you will resurrect a fun pastime. I can hear you ask "That's all very well and good, but how did it contribute toward your personal development?"

I will provide two examples which I painted during the personal development phase of my foundation course. These pictures added to the work I was going through at the time. As I have written earlier, at the start of my foundation year I was mourning the death of my mother and in a job that was beginning to strangle me. This meant that I was very guarded and quiet for the first couple of months of the course. You can see my state of mind at that point in Figure 5.1. Nothing really occurred to me as I was painting this but when I stood back and looked at it, I was shocked by the sense of darkness and oppression it portrayed to me. It might reflect something different for you but for me it was overwhelmingly negative. Picture number two (Figure 5.2) is indicative of a different mind-set and was painted toward the end of my foundation year. At this point I had decided that counselling was the career for me. I was less rigid, more communicative and open. For me, it reflects emancipation. I roughly knew the state of my mind while painting both pictures but they both affirmed my feelings in a way words never could. Art is not for everyone but it can be a nice addition to your personal development tool kit.

Figure 5.1.

Figure 5.2.

Final thoughts

All of this personal development stuff can seem a bit self-obsessed and narcissistic. However, the crucial difference here is the motivation behind personal development: the client and your role as a counsellor. I don't think many people would jump at the chance to examine their shadow side. Most people don't want see their negative aspects and I understand that, it can be very uncomfortable.

Summary

- Find an accredited counsellor whom you like but also one that will challenge you and help in your personal development.
- Try out different types of therapy if you can.
- Keep a journal to record your thoughts and emotions on a daily basis.
- Give art a chance. It doesn't matter how good you are as long as it means something to you.

Chapter Six
Class participation; working in dyads and triads

Dyads and triads

The extent of practical experience varies from course to course. I really enjoyed the chance to practice counselling skills with my class mates; it was through this practice that I realised I really liked this counselling business. If you are considering a few courses right now, ask the course directors about the amount of time dedicated to practicing counselling skills. In my opinion, more academic courses with little emphasis on counselling skills will not prepare you for the real thing.

The only way to practice is in twos (dyad; one counsellor and one client) or threes (triad; counsellor, client and observer). Actually, there is a dreaded third, which is called the fish bowl. In the fish bowl you act as counsellor and client for 20 minutes each, in front of your class and a tutor, who grades your counselling skills. You won't experience that in your foundation year so you can relax (for now). The dyad is good for starters, particularly if you are in anyway nervous about this, which you probably will be. Normally, each practice session will last 10 minutes, after which you will swap roles and practice for a further 10 minutes. You and your practice partner will most likely be asked for your feedback; this is for each other and for the benefit of the class, at the end of the session. I find practicing in triads the most useful. In these situations each pair of counsellor/client is observed by a third class mate. Note is taken of things that went well as well as any obvious mistakes made by the counsellor. As with dyad practice, roles are swapped after a fixed period of time until each participant has had a chance to be counsellor, client and observer. At the end of the session all three participants are invited to provide constructive feedback.

It is difficult to overcome the awkwardness of these sessions at first, particularly when you don't really know your classmates. These are intimate sessions and people can be very anxious about being somehow assessed by the observer. Eventually, it will become second nature and you will grow to relish the chance to practice your skills (if counselling is for you).

There is one particular reason why I find triads more informative than dyads and that is the presence of the observer. Each of us has a blind spot, unseen by ourselves and those close to us. This phenomenon is best described by a device known as the Johari Window.

The Johari Window[4]

This device is used to illustrate and highlight the notion of blind spots. It is comprised of 4 squares. As you can see from the illustration in Figure 6.1, each individual possesses two blind spots. The first is where behaviours and characteristics are unknown to you but known to others (bottom left square of figure 6.1).

The second and potentially more insidious blind spot can be seen on the bottom right of the window, where thoughts, emotions and wants remain hidden from both you as we'll as others. This is the area most commonly investigated by a counsellor and often picked up by the observer when practising in triads. In my opinion, this area only becomes illuminated by some sudden flash of insight or with the help of a counsellor.

	Known to self	Unknown to self
Known to others	Shared awareness	Blind to self but known to others
Unknown to others	Private self	Unknown to self and others; unconscious

Figure 6.1. Johari window. Reflects different aspects of the self that are known by the self and others. The lower right quadrant is often the area investigated in counselling and psychotherapy.

---

[4] The word Johari is a composite of the forenames of the two men who devised the tool: Joseph Luft and Harrington Ingham. The concept was first published in the *Proceedings of the Western Training Laboratory in Group Development* in 1950.

Class discussions

I am very lucky to have class mates of diverse backgrounds and experiences that help me learn and develop as a result of class discussions. Occasionally, these discussions get heated; people have different opinions and can be very passionate about them. In general, we respect each other and accept what can be challenging issues. I learn so much from throwing an idea into the centre of the room to be teased apart and reassembled by my classmates. A lot of my ideas and opinions may be wrong but by deconstructing them in class I can test and learn how they are wrong or where they might fit into counselling theory. Try to engage in class discussion; providing you feel safe with your peers in the room, you'll get a lot out of it.

Basic Counselling Skills

Here is a list of the principle counselling skills you will practice in class with your peers:

Active listening
When you actively listen to someone you show that person that you are interested and engaged in what they are saying. You are **present**. You pay attention with your **body language** and gestures. Remember details. Ask **clarifying questions**. **Reflect** back to your client what you heard. Provide **summaries** of what you heard at regular junctures.

Advanced Empathy
This is more than trying to step into the others shoes, which is equally important. With advanced empathy the counsellor helps with implied feelings.

For example, the counsellor might say:

"I notice every time you mention your work colleague, you wince and cross your arms."

A client might not have been aware about this and realise that this colleague is causing distress, which was heretofore largely unconscious.

Open questioning
Counsellors avoid direct closed questions, which can give the impression to the client that he or she is being judged. Closed questions often limit people to yes or no answers.

An example of a closed question:

"Don't you think you drink too much?"
Open questions can be just as effective and tend not to raise defences:

"Might your drinking be impacting on your family life?"

Challenging
An important counselling skill used to highlight blind spots or distorted thinking.

Example response to a client with low self-esteem:

"I notice you believe you are unintelligent and stupid, however I have heard you talk about your degree and participation on a number of committees."

One final point, followed by a word of caution: when your skills are being assessed, it is the client and his or her story that makes the practicing counsellor look good in front of tutors. Do your classmates a favour and bring your best issues to the fore when you are playing the client to their counsellor. Finally, be careful not to bring something so traumatic to your practice that you can't remain attentive for the rest of the class. This happens from time to time but try to get a sense of when this is likely to occur and take the appropriate action.

Summary

- Dyads and triads are common ways of practicing counselling skills with class mates.
- The Johari window is a useful way to illustrate unconscious elements (blind spots) hidden from the client as well as family and friends.
- Participate in class discussion as much as possible; you will miss it when it's gone.
- Bring real issues to practice (but nothing that is too traumatic).

Reading list

- The Skilled Helper: A Problem-Management and Opportunity-Development Approach to Helping by Gerard Egan
- Theory and Practice of Counseling and Psychotherapy by Gerald Corey

Chapter Seven
Assignments

The dreaded word: essay. For me, it conjures up the smell of chalk and dusty black boards, panic over lack of preparation, as well as the apathy of the young college student hell bent on having a good time at the expense of the obligatory assignment. I have (had) one foot in academia and research, so I am no stranger to writing papers on my work. Nevertheless, I was anxious about writing essays in the context of counselling and psychotherapy. Perhaps it was the fact that I was back in a school-like setting and all the baggage of judgement that comes with it. I can't imagine how daunting it must have been for some of my class mates, some of whom hadn't written an essay since school, thirty years hence.

I am not in the position to lecture you on how to gain top marks for the perfect assignment and I haven't always received top grades. What I can do is provide you with my approach to writing essays and share the mistakes I made so that you can avoid them when writing yours.

Formative and summative essays

Formative essays are all about personal development and direct personal experience related to the assignment topic. You don't need to have supporting references nor detailed accounts of theories and approaches to counselling in these essays. It's all about bearing your soul in the appropriate context. This is where your journal and your little black book (described earlier) will come in very handy. Change your focus slightly the moment you start your new module so that your antennae are ready to pick up any relevant ideas. Often, important ideas pop into your head as you're waiting for the bus or vacuuming your house. Likewise, use the work you do with your personal counsellor, who should be able to help with any blind spots you may have around the topic in question. Be as honest and open as you can. Write it for yourself and your own development and forget about grades.

Unfortunately for the summative essays, you will have to worry about the grades because this is where the craft of writing essays comes into play, as much as your knowledge of the topic. There is no point in being an aficionado on Freud if you don't know how to structure a basic essay. Like the formative essay, your journaling and other notebooks will be very useful with its summative counterpart. A summative essay differs from the formative in a number of different ways and the level of sophistication required depends upon your year of study. Your college or university should have guides as to what is expected from your essays as you progress through your course. Obviously first year essays are much less involved than those required for the final year of a degree program.

Summative essays are almost always based on an academic topic, from theories and theorists to ethics and the law. You will have to read books, research articles and reputable academic websites (Wikipedia won't do I'm afraid), all of which must be referenced correctly and appropriately. It can be a scary prospect but it doesn't have to be. In the following section I will outline the steps and methods I use when preparing for and writing a summative essay. It may not be the best way but it generally works for me and even if it doesn't work for you, you can always learn from my mistakes.

Read the question

It is very important that you understand exactly what your tutor and your college expects in a good essay. Ask them if you are unsure; don't assume you know what they want. Read the essay requirements carefully and deconstruct it into its various components (Figure 7.1). Write these components at the start of your essay and go back to them at regular intervals and ask yourself "Am I sticking to the essay requirements?" Don't go off and write an essay based on what you're really interested in. For example, if the narrative requires an essay about the relationship between Carl Jung and spirituality, don't you go off and write a lovely essay about the role of Buddhism in psychotherapy. I have thankfully caught myself veering down that road a number of times. To conclude: read the question!

"Third Year trainees will be in the process of forming a flexible and informed ethical sense that will guide them in their performance of their role as counsellor or psychotherapist". **Discuss**

"Third Year trainees will be in the process of forming a flexible and informed ethical sense that will guide them in their performance of their role as counsellor or psychotherapist".

'in the process'

Does this imply continuous education regarding ethics and the law? Should students and qualified counsellors be up to date on the law regarding counselling? Do you agree. Discuss.

'forming a flexible informed ethical sense'

What does flexible mean when engaging ethically with your clients?

'forming an Informed ethical sense'

How would you go about informing yourself? What source would you use? What is the current position regarding counselling and the law?

performance of their role as counsellor

How might you link the law and ethics into your practice as a counsellor? What supports could you use? Supervision, peer support, regulatory bodies?

Figure 7.1. Deconstruct your essay question into its important constituents. Write notes regarding how you might address these different sections. Refer to this plan as you write your essay to make sure you stay on track.

Make a master plan

Some people are very clever and don't need a plan. Once the literature is read they can start the essay and complete it from the basic structure of it that lies in their head. Sadly I'm not that clever; I need a plan. I usually begin with a master plan, which outlines the basic structure of the essay, from the title down to the conclusion (Figure 7.2) and then subdivide these main areas into smaller sections, which are also planned, right down to individual paragraphs if I have to. With practice you won't need as much planning but if writing essays is a long distant memory for you, then a lot of planning can help ground you and stave off any rising panic.

As you can see from figure 7.2, the basic structure is relatively obvious. You start with title, table of contents, abstract if required, introduction, main headings of your story and finish with a conclusion and your references. However, before you sit down to write your masterpiece you will need to read the relevant literature.

Literature Review

Use your notebook, carry it with you everywhere and note down your ideas for essay topics or the structure of the essay when they pop into our head. Get access to the appropriate books and articles and read as many as you can (within reason). Ask your tutors for advice on titles as well as any other requirements such as the number of references expected (i.e. do you need to read 10 books or just 5). I have made the mistake of not checking with my tutors whether my chosen essay title was appropriate or not. Remember the tutor is normally the person who will grade your essay. Find out what he or she expects and comply.

The Internet, YouTube and apps

I found writing essays in the humanities (e.g. Counselling and Psychotherapy) much more free than writing about medical research. Check with your tutors but you should be free to quote reputable websites and associated teaching videos on YouTube as well as the usual books and research articles (Figure 7.3). Use the Internet wisely and avoid websites that are not linked with institutions of professional bodies. You can subscribe to the counselling channel on YouTube which gives lots of video tutorials from experts and students. YouTube can also be a big help when looking for documentaries on the masters of psychotherapy such as Freud, Jung, Rogers and Beck. There a few apps on the market that can help with essays, some of which include the free 'iTunes U', an app that provides tutorials and lectures on up to date topics from a number of universities worldwide. 'TED talks' can also be very illuminating. TED stands for technology, entertainment and design and represents a non-profit organisation that arranges talks from world experts on a huge number of topics. The talks can be accessed directly from their website (www.ted.com), YouTube or via app, all of which are free to access.

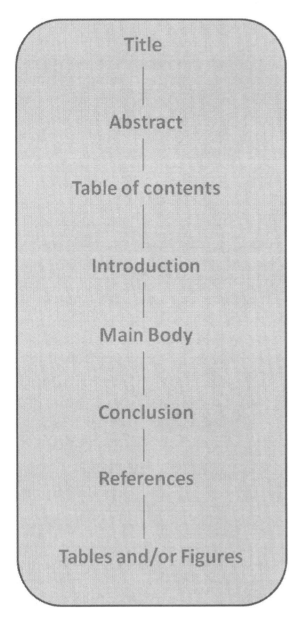

Figure 7.2. The basic structure of an essay.

Books

Don't forget the humble book and your local library, which can be the most useful and first port of call for any student. You will find a book on Freud in almost any library, no matter how small. There are also a number ways to get our hands on cheap second hand books such as the online book seller Amazon. Search for your book on amazon.com, once you find it click on the 'used' button underneath the price and you will find a number of second hand book dealers selling your book for a fraction of the cost of a new book. I have used this on numerous occasions in the past and the books, although used, are always in good condition. If you're a fan of e-readers such as the kindle or Sony reader then you can avail of eLibraries on the Internet that will rent you out books (Figure 7.3).

Once you have found your reading material use your trusty pencil to take note of the salient points that stick out for you. Always have your master plan to hand in order to check that you're staying on course and don't get bogged down in irrelevant areas. In the end, you will have pages of notes that are ready to be sculpted and moulded to fit the scaffold of your master plan.

Essay Introduction

Try to capture the reader's imagination with the first sentence. For example: "When surveyed, more than 85% of adolescent American males said they consumed Internet pornography at least once a week." Try to set the stage. Tell the reader why you chose this topic and provide some personal information if appropriate. For example: "I have seen a young male client as part of my clinical placement who frequently consumes internet pornography." Follow this personal information with a brief outline on what you will discuss and what you aim to achieve.

Main body

This is where you provide examples of current thinking on the subject area, which includes principle theories as well as research of past and current experts. Order these paragraphs from early work, right up to contemporary studies. If appropriate, try and divide the literature into those that agree versus those that disagree with the premise of your essay. For example: there are research papers written by counsellors who believe that pornography consumption does engender misogynistic thinking as well those who report the opposite point of view. Unless specifically asked to in your narrative, avoid taking sides. Just present the literature as you find it. Next, summarise the findings by giving the apparent pros and cons of each point of view.

At this point, your understanding of the essay narrative comes into play. Are you required to provide personal opinion on the topic? Are you asked to write about how this topic relates to your role as a counsellor or simply to provide an unbiased, simple review of the literature? This is where I have fallen in the past.

Extra information sources:

The counselling channel on YouTube
http://www.youtube.com/user/CounsellingChannel

iTunesU for iPhone and iPad
The iTunes U app gives you access to complete courses from leading universities and other schools plus the world's largest digital catalogue of free education content .

TED talks
www.ted.com

Used books from amazon.com

Questia allows you to view books online for a monthly fee www.questia.com

Internet Text Archive
http://archive.org/details.php?identifier=texts

If you have a **Kindle eReader** you can rent text books from Amazon (www.amazon.com)

Borrow books from **The Open Library** at openlibrary.org/borrow

Figure 7.3. Useful websites and apps that might act as useful sources for your essay writing.

Conclusion

Don't just repeat word for word what you wrote in the main section. Start by saying whether you achieved the objectives laid out at the end of your introduction or not. State that the literature provides arguments for and against the subject matter. If appropriate, give your opinion regarding future work e.g. "Prospective studies need to be carried out in order to examine the attitudes of adolescent males who consume internet pornography over a 10 year period."   No matter how sure you are about whether the research findings or theories are right or wrong; never state that something is definitively 'this' or 'that'. It is almost impossible to categorically prove that anything is absolutely correct when studying the elusive mind and human behaviour. Be humble and use phrases like 'might be' or 'it is likely that'.

The Nuts and bolts

The paragraph

A paragraph is a microcosm of your essay as a whole. It should have a beginning, middle and end. Each paragraph should lead smoothly into the next one. For this reason the very first and last sentences of each paragraph are very important. In general, the last sentence of the preceding paragraph should introduce the subject of the subsequent one.

Grammar

I recommend reading 'Eats, Shoots and Leaves' by Lynne Truss. Grammar is a particular failing of mine so I have found that book helpful. It is a treasure trove of information and quite funny to boot. Read it and see how many grammatical and punctuation errors I have made in this book!

Words

Don't try and introduce multi-syllabic words for the sake of it. You might think it makes you sound very learned indeed but they can be distracting and unnecessary if applied inappropriately. I try to write as if I am explaining the concept to my mother who is (was) unfamiliar with the topic. This always forced me to keep my writing as clear as I could. It doesn't always work (as you can probably see from reading this book!) but it can be a useful rule of thumb. Remember, clarity is king. Get a thesaurus and use it. Avoid repeating words (if you can) in the once sentence

Sentences

Short and clear sentences beat long meandering ones every time. Be as economical as you can with your words and sentences. Try to get your point across in as few words as possible. Imagine that each word costs you €1/£1/$1 or whatever currency you use and try not to spend all your money writing the essay!

Quotations

This can be a tricky area. Too little and it can look like you haven't read a thing. Too much and it appears as if you simply cut and pasted your entire essay from the work of others. Treat quotations like birds eye chillies and use them sparingly! Try not to quote entire paragraphs, just the most relevant sentences.

Referencing

The most common reference style used in the humanities is Harvard style. You can find examples of this style everywhere on the internet and in many articles and books. The University of Exeter in the UK, provide an excellent guide on how to use Harvard referencing (http://education.exeter.ac.uk/dll/studyskills/harvard_referencing.htm). The other common style is that of the American Psychological Association (APA), the details of which can be found on their website: www.apastyle.org.

For your convenience here is an example of the basic Harvard style when referencing a book by a fictional author, Peter Murphy:

Murphy, P. 2013. Studying counselling is fun. 2nd Edition, Dublin, Sage

There are software packages out there that will automatically generate your bibliographies for you, which include *EndNote* and *Reference Manager*. They are very useful tools if you can access them. More advanced editions of Microsoft Word also possess a basic reference manager option.

Remember that every time you write a sentence that is based on someone else's writing, even if it's not a direct quote, you must reference it.

For example: "Murphy has shown that counselling can be fun (Murphy, 2013)."

Kill your babies!

We all occasionally write paragraphs that we are very proud of. On reading back to ourselves we can hardly believe we wrote such a great piece! If that paragraph fits into your essay then you can leave it in with pride. On the other hand, if it bears no relation to the essay topic, you must delete it.

Formatting

Microsoft Word has a number of themes you can use to help you with formatting your essay. As a general rule, use common fonts like Arial, Times New Roman or Calibri. Headings should be 16, subheadings 14 and the main text 12 but you can use Word to help you with this. Align the text to both left and right margins by 'justifying' it. Insert page numbers and if appropriate, use headings to include your name and the title of your essay. Personally, I think you should be artistic with your cover page and introduce some of your personality into it. Again, Microsoft Word has a number of 'Cover Page' design templates you can use. Don't be afraid to add colour and grab your reader's attention.

A picture is worth a thousand words

If you can, add pretty pictures, tables or figures to illustrate your point. Just make sure they're relevant to your essay topic.

Leave your masterpiece to cool down

Once you have written your draft, leave it alone for at least two days. Don't look at it or think about it. When you eventually go back and read it you will have a fresh and clear perspective. The mistakes will be more apparent. View your sentences like small hedges that need to be pruned in order to get them just right.

Be disciplined

Nothing can strike fear in a person like a looming deadline. Sometimes I'm good at getting things done on time, other times I procrastinate at an Olympic level. A simple cure for this malaise is to follow this rule: 'I will write 250 words per day, no matter how daft or irrelevant they might seem at the time.' It's far better to cut back your essay than to add words to it. If you get into this habit you will be surprised at how much you can accumulate over a week. It's all about momentum; once you have started its easier to continue.

Ask someone to read your essay before submitting

Whether it's a friend, family member or class mate, get someone to read your masterpiece before submitting it. It doesn't matter if your friend doesn't know anything about Freud. Ask them to check readability, spelling and grammar. My college has a reading service, where tutors will read your essay for a fee. If you're unsure about your essay and your university or college provides this service, use it.

A final word on plagiarism

Be careful about plagiarising your sources of information – in other words, don't do it! You can get into a lot of trouble with plagiarism, even if you do it unconsciously, which isn't as uncommon as you might think. Always scan your drafts for plagiarism. I know it can be hard sometimes not to write almost exactly what someone else has written, particularly if it's a clear piece of writing. After all, there are only so many ways you can say something.

Nevertheless, you must try and re-write the concept in your own words. It will get easier with practice.

Summary

- Read the essay question or narrative very carefully – deconstruct it and make a plan
- Carry a notebook around to record your ideas
- Stick to your plan and constantly refer back to it
- Use the internet and apps as well as more traditional sources of information
- Be economic with your language
- Make sure your paragraphs have a beginning, middle and end
- Ensure your paragraphs lead into each other
- Put your essay to one side for a few days then re-read it
- Ask someone else to read your essay
- Use quotations and references appropriately
- Figures and tables can enhance your essay

Reading list

- Eats, Shoots and Leaves by Lynne Truss

Chapter Eight
Self-care and Support

Peer support is without peer

I have mentioned elsewhere that your personal counsellor should be a source of support and challenge, someone who helps you develop yourself as a more whole human being. You probably will only meet your counsellor once a week at most and due to professional boundaries you won't be able to call him or her for a chat about how you're feeling on any particular day; likewise with your supervisor. The supervisor/counsellor relationship is more distant than that with your personal counsellor.

Unfortunately, you won't be able to discuss your clients or how you feel about difficult cases with friends and family, without breaking through a myriad of ethical and professional boundaries. I miss not being able to come home after a hard day's work and launching into a mild rant about a difficult work colleague to my partner. As a counsellor you can't do that, and rightly so. However, that leaves you in a rather difficult and lonely position. It's ironic; you will spend your time listening to people discuss their lives (which is always a great privilege) and at the end of the day there is nobody for you to talk to. Occasionally, I have come home bursting at the seams with a need to share what I have experienced, but I can't.

Who can you turn to?

Your peers, particularly your class mates, can be a great source of comfort on such occasions. They know your position. In fact, they are probably experiencing similar emotions at the same time. You don't discuss the personal details of any case but you can share feelings, thoughts and frustrations. You will miss your classmates when school ends during the summer or after you qualify. As I write this chapter, I have finished third year and am preparing to enter the final year of my degree. In fourth year we get to specialise into our chosen fields and so our class will be broken up and mixed with other groups. Some of my class mates have decided to defer this final year (as things stand in Ireland you can practice after obtaining your diploma). As a result, I won't have the close peer support I have come to rely upon. We as a class realise the importance of peer support and so have decided to meet up once a month. Of course, you will be closer to some class mates than others and will probably meet those peers more frequently. Make sure you retain our peer support throughout your studies and afterwards.

Take time away from school

As much as you will rely upon peer support you still need a break from them and your course. Make an effort to engage in life outside of counselling; immerse yourself in exercise, hobbies, family and friends.

If you can, meditate

I mentioned in the last section how my inner voice occasionally wags its finger at me, telling me how I need to meditate more. Meditation is one of the most effective ways for me to manage my thoughts and emotions. If I can, I like to mediate between each client; it helps me prepare my mind for the next person. I have already devoted a lot of space in this book to Mindfulness, as a form of psychotherapy. The reality is that mindfulness shouldn't be regarded as merely therapy, it should be thought of as breakfast; without it, your mind will be hungry and grumpy. You don't have to be a devotee of the Dalai Lama or an ascetic monk in the hills of northern India to meditate. It's enough to quieten your mind for a minimum of ten minutes each day. It's not a sport, so you don't have to measure up to anyone else. You accept everything in your life as it is for those ten minutes. Accept all thoughts and emotions and watch them float by without judging them. Our minds are like a car engine that is constantly revving. Your brain never ceases streaming out billions of thoughts over a lifetime, one after another; some relevant, others not so much. If you spend ten minutes in silence, you allow the engine to idle and relieve the relentless pressure it must be under. Doing so can only prolong the life time of the vehicle. Many, many research studies have been carried out by serious research institutions into the physical benefits of daily mediation from reducing your risk of heart disease to enhancing the capacity of your immune system to eliminate infections.

Here is a quick list of other stress busting activities:

- Try to get some physical exercise daily.

- Engage socially if you can with friends, family or in social clubs.

- If you have any free time left you could do worse than engaging in some sort of charity. Studies have shown that aiding those less fortunate than ourselves can alleviate depression and bring fresh perspective.

- Eat as healthily as you can.

- Engage more with your pets. If you don't have one, think about getting one.

- You won't have the time to engage in many of the above (I certainly don't) but know that they are all proven and effective ways to relieve tension. Burn out does happen, so don't think you're immune. Try to have fun whenever you can.

Chapter Nine
Clinical placement

Let's dispense with this notion that only a select few of us suffer and therefore require counselling and psychotherapy. We all suffer; each and every one of us. It is the very nature of what it means to be human and the act that levels all playing fields. I used to think that my family was the only one that had issues. I would cycle home from friend's houses as a kid and think to myself "Why can't my family be like that?" Of course the truth is that there is no such thing as a perfect family, only the varying grades of turbulent relationships, driven by long forgotten hurts and neglects committed by each member; likewise with personal suffering. Yes, some people suffer more than others but that doesn't alter the fact that we all suffer.

As a society (I can only speak for my own in Ireland), we haven't quite got the hang of admitting such weaknesses yet to our fellow man or woman. Many of us (including myself at one time or another) believe it stoic and necessary to deny suffering and frailty. We forget that to face into the abyss of pain that lies within can represent courage secondary only to facing death itself. That's what counselling really is: to face into your own personal darkness and suffering, persevere through your own dark night of the soul and come out the other side a more accepting, forgiving and open human being. As I said at the start of the book, you don't need to have suffered to be a counsellor, but it helps. The good news is that since we all suffer, we all have the capacity to cultivate empathy and compassion for fellow human beings in need. And that is precisely what you will need to bring to your clinical placement.

Finding a placement

This will depend on your college or university. Some courses might provide placements for their students in charities, agencies or government controlled institutes and hospitals. We weren't so lucky in our course and had to fend for ourselves for the most part. I think this policy is a mistake and places more pressure on students than is necessary; students will be stressed enough about starting their clinical placement without the prospect of walking the streets looking for a placement. Once again, I was lucky to be helped by one of my tutors, who recommended me to a busy medical practice as a low cost counsellor. This was perfect for me and meant that I was exposed to a wide variety of clients with different needs and issues. For some of my class mates it was a little harder. They had to go out into the big bad world and look for a placement. Many ended up working for charities that specialised in specific areas such as suicide, gay and lesbian issues or addiction. Others tried advertising in local community centres as low cost counsellors.

My advice to you is to be proactive and explore your options early. If you have an interest in a particular type of counselling then seek out the relevant agencies and ask to meet with coordinators and counsellors already working there. Canvas the opinion of local doctors; ask them if they have a space to rent in their clinic or if they would refer patients to you.

Supervision

Supervision and finding the right supervisor was a frequent topic of debate amongst my class mates. We all had similar enough experiences, which weren't always positive. Supervision is not like personal counselling, it's generally more directive and less comfortable. Several of my class mates felt that their supervisors were overly directive and often critical, which seemed to fly against our preconceived notions of counselling and counsellors. Personally, while I found it a world away from personal counselling I did find supervision useful a lot of the time. However, it is more like being in a class room than a counselling room. I frequently sat with my notebook at the ready to take down suggestions about dealing with this or that client. Sometimes the advice I received missed the mark. I think it must be hard for supervisors to dole out advice on a client they haven't met. It seems to me that advice can only be given in relation to you (the counsellor) and how you are dealing with your own issues in relation to your client. In other words, supervision should be about keeping you on the straight and narrow, identifying your transferences and the emergence of your shadow side. You will need to talk about times when you might feel anger against your client because they perhaps remind you of a difficult person from your past or present. Often, these shadow elements remain in the unconscious, far removed from your waking, logical mind/brain complex. Your goal is not to let your own issues interfere with the progress of your client in their counselling; your supervisor can be very helpful with such issues.

Your first day

Most people remember their first day at school, their first boyfriend or girlfriend and their first day in a new job; your first day as a trainee counsellor is no less momentous. Up until this point you will have studied the different schools and practiced in dyads and triads with your class mates but in truth, nothing can prepare you for the real thing. My head was filled with the plans I had for how to deal with all sorts of clients. I would adopt CBT for one type of client, mindfulness with another and so on. I rehearsed the different options in my head during the day and before I went to sleep. I had my contract ready (more about the contract later) and my intake forms.

I was literally shaking at the knees, waiting for my first client. I was in an empty doctor's room, which are a bit clinical (as one might expect!) and not the most appropriate for counselling, when the call came through that my first client had arrived. I went out (jelly legged) to the waiting room and invited my first client (ever) to follow me into the room. We sat and I was about to introduce myself and the type of counselling on offer, when the client just started talking. She didn't stop for 20 minutes. I was metaphorically blown back into my seat by the force of her emotion. Schools of therapy went out the window, as did everything else inside my head. It occurred to me in a flash that my role as a counsellor was first and foremost to **shut up and listen**. My nerves dissipated immediately. Obviously at later sessions I got to suggest different methods of relaxation, thought record sheets and other aspects of psychotherapy but for the first two sessions or so I simply listened to her story. It has pretty much been the same for each new client since. So, be calm, centred, sit back and listen without interruption.

Details, details, details

Your clients will often flood your brain with hundreds of names, dates, places and objects during the course of these first few sessions. I believe that you should try and remember as many of these details as possible. Your notes are invaluable in this regard. The moment your client leaves, take out your notebook and jot down names, dates and places mentioned during the session. Many clients (including myself) feel listened to when the counsellor remembers the names of important people as well as the time lines associated with their stories.

Resist the urge to fix and dole out advice

It is not your place to fix. As a counsellor, you are there to listen and facilitate change in your client, by constantly reflecting back their stories and behaviour in the room. I have noticed that every time I jump in to fix, I tend to be far from the mark and can in some cases irk my client. Carl Rogers admitted that he frequently didn't know how he was going to help a client during initial sessions. If one of the great luminaries of psychotherapy in the 20th century admits to fallibility, then a lowly, inexperienced counsellor such as me should also take heed. Of course this opinion will mean little to you if you are firmly entrenched in one of the more directive schools such as REBT, and that's fine; go with the type of psychotherapy that fits you.

Review and summarise

Frequent reviews can help clients chart their progress and bring forgotten aspects of their stories into greater perspective. You will find that clients will tell their stories over and over again. It's as if they are orbiting their issues like the earth revolving around the sun. Each revolution provides a different perspective and reveals new insights.

Ending therapy can be as illuminating as starting it.

Therapy generally doesn't last forever; sooner or later the client must leave, hopefully better prepared to face future issues. You will probably know when therapy is coming to an end. The topics discussed in sessions tend to take the form of a normal conversation. At this point, it might be prudent to flag to your client that therapy is approaching its natural end. In my limited experience I have found that clients do not like these conversations. They will have become used to their one hour weekly sessions in which they can discuss their issues in safety. I have been in this position as a client and it is scary, no matter how much progress you have made or how well equipped you are to face the world. Nevertheless, this ending phase can be very productive. Deeply embedded issues tend to emerge near the end, which can lead to rapid personal progress. This period is also a very good way to examine how your client (and you as a counsellor) behaves in similar circumstances outside the counselling room. I for one have always found goodbyes difficult; I tend to disappear into the night, in an attempt to avoid an emotional farewell.

You should also use this period to discuss their plans for maintaining a healthy mind in the absence of a weekly counselling session. Write these contingency plans down together if you can.

Contracts

There are plenty of examples of contracts online. Some counsellors don't like them and feel that it gives the wrong impression to the client, while others see it as essential. I have provided an example of a contract that I use in Figure 9.1. This contract is based on one devised by my tutor for *ethics in counselling*.

Many counsellors promise absolute confidentiality in their promotional material and on their website. This is true for the most part, however, there are exceptions. The principle one being if your client identifies himself or another who plans to cause harm to a member of the public (the example frequently provided is acts of terrorism). In Ireland we have a Children First policy whereby the relevant authorities are encouraged to report any indications of child abuse, mental or physical. While this is an important policy, it is not yet law in Ireland (2013) and so counsellors are not bound to comply with it. You must use your own judgement and seek advice from your supervisor and governing body in such cases.

Notes

When I started my clinical placement, my notes were similar to a novel written by one of the Bronte sisters in the Victorian era. I soon stopped this, as it would have completely consumed the time I had in between clients. It's important to leave enough time between sessions so you can gather yourself and prepare for the next session, as well as ensuring that clients don't bump into each other on their way in and out.

These days, I jot down the salient points, including important names and dates. I try to write my notes as if the client could ask to read them at any juncture, which they can. It is important to write respectful and informative summaries of your sessions.

You should code your client's names in your notes and store them in a secure location. Often, client intake sheets are stored separately, also in a secure location. For example, I store mine on a rolodex in a lockable cash box. You can decide how best to code your clients names yourself; you must ensure that someone can't simply pick up your notes and recognise the names of those concerned. I'm not going to give you my coding system but you could use something like the date of your first session together, followed by the clients initials turned backwards. For example, if I was your client, your code for me might be 170513DP (the date followed my initials reversed). It doesn't matter how you do it, as long as you do it.

Personally, I like to have an electronic back up of my notes. I either write or type my notes onto a computer and store them in the "cloud" as well as on separate hard drive that gets stored away in my lockable box. I find Microsoft OneNote, which is part of any standard Microsoft Office package, very useful. You can password protect each file in OneNote, which acts as a secondary fail safe mechanism for keeping your notes secure. Each of my clients has their own folder in OneNote, which is password protected with back-ups stored in the cloud as well as on a hard drive. That might be overkill on my part but I like the security of it all. There also numerous apps out there for apple and android users which allow easy note taking on tablets, phones and other devices, such as Evernote, Notability and UPad.

Counsellor – Client Agreement

xxxxxxx is a qualified counsellor who has received his diploma in Counselling and Psychotherapy from xxxxxxx.

What is counselling?

- The purpose of counselling is to provide a safe, confidential place wherein you can safely talk about the losses, stresses, confusion, conflicts and other pain in your life.
- My role as a counsellor is to listen, support and help you with theoretical insight in order to change what is possible or to live more contentedly and creatively with that which is not. As a counsellor I will not judge your thoughts, feelings or behaviour. I do not give advice, make diagnoses or prognoses. My goal is to help empower you, the client, to find your own solutions and to ensure that you have the tools to deal with difficult situations should they arise again in the future.
- It is important to note that emotional pain may initially increase after commencement of counselling.

Confidentiality

- Our work will be confidential, **except** in the event that you identify any person who intends to cause harm to a member of the public.
- I am obliged to attend a supervisor on a weekly basis. The supervisor's role is to ensure that I as your counsellor can offer you the best possible assistance. I will discuss your case with this supervisor but will not reveal your identity.

The counselling agreement includes the following:

- Each session will last one hour and cost XXX
- If you are late, the session will still end one hour after the appointed time.
- Cancellation where necessary will be notified at least 24 hours prior to the appointed time.
- I keep regular notes, which you are entitled to see at any stage.
- Due to the nature of my work I am not available between sessions or at weekends.
- Should I meet you outside of this office, you will dictate the absence or presence of a greeting.
- You are entitled to terminate counselling at any time and without explanation, should you find our working together not helpful.

Signed: _____   Client signature: _____

Figure 9.1. An example of Counsellor – Client agreement

Ethical dilemma notebook

This book isn't intended to be an encyclopaedia of counselling and as I have said repeatedly, I am no expert. However, I feel it is important to recommend that you keep a notebook in which you log any ethical dilemmas encountered during your placement and beyond. We had an excellent tutor for ethics and the law and he advised that we keep such a notebook. You can log any dilemmas you might encounter in any session into it. You will need to show that you dealt with such problems in a systematic and logical way and that you brought such issues to your supervisor. That way, in the very unlikely event that a client or third party should wish to take legal action against you, you will be prepared. I'm not recommending this to scare you and I don't want to give the impression that counselling is all about covering your behind. It's important for all concerned that you show that you operate in a professional manner. You should read Tim Bond's book on ethics and the law in counselling for more information, particularly in relation to client autonomy.

Autonomy simply means that as citizens we have the right to make decisions and carry out actions without interference, providing our actions do not harm other citizens. In most cases, your client's right to autonomy takes precedence. Exceptions might include circumstances where a client has explicit and concrete plans to hurt other people, such as acts of terrorism. In such scenarios you are obliged to contact the relevant authorities.

Insurance

My College covers all students for professional indemnity insurance (should a client or third party take legal action against you) as long as they remain students. However, we are on our own once we finish and have to get your own. If your college doesn't provide such insurance, you need to get some and make sure any policy covers accidental injury if you are operating from your home or rented premises. Governing bodies are normally helpful in suggesting reputable companies.

Self-care

Try to enjoy your placement; it is after all why you embarked on your studies in the first place. Practice self-care for the sake of you and your client. Find ways to relax and shed the many strong emotions you have been exposed to during the day. Use your peers and supervision to help guide you in difficult scenarios. Engage in as many non-counselling activities as possible. Enjoy your family, friends and past times. If you do this you will be better equipped to help those who need their stories heard.

Summary

- Resist the urge to fix your client. You can't.

- Find the supervisor you deserve – one that makes you work.

- Generate a contract that is very clear about what confidentiality means.

- Keep clear, concise notes in a secure environment, separate from your client intake forms.

- Code your client's names.

- Write your notes as if you expect them to be read by another party.

- Keep a notebook in which to record ethical dilemmas.

Reading list

- Standards and Ethics for Counselling in Action by Tim Bond.

Chapter Ten
An Interview with a student of counselling and psychotherapy: Mary Mahon

Mary is a remarkable 62 year old woman who has experienced significant loss and hardship throughout her life. Importantly, Mary granted me permission to reveal her age in this chapter, which I think is very relevant to many prospective student counsellors. I hope those reading this, who believe they lack the required academic skills or feel they are too old to embark on a new career, gain encouragement from Mary's story.

 Mary became widowed at a young age and was left to successfully rear her family on her own; these days she is a proud mother of 7 children and 3 step children and grandmother to 13 grandchildren (and counting). Sadly, Mary's son died in a tragic accident during the second year of her counselling degree and her mother passed away one year later. Anyone else might have succumbed to grief and deferred their studies but Mary persevered with her work as a student counsellor. As a friend and classmate, I found her singular strength and depth of character humbling to behold. In spite of these tragedies, she worked through her sadness and pain, attended all her modules, completed all assignments and is now a qualified counsellor.

 I have been lucky to engage with Mary in various dyads and triads, where we were obliged to test our counselling skills. I always found her gentle and attentive nature immediately disarming. She simply listens and by doing so goes a long way to healing the suffering of whoever sits in front of her. I always left our practice sessions together a little lighter. Despite her enormous wealth of life experience, Mary entered the degree program lacking in confidence, particularly in relation to the academic aspects of the course. She has relayed to me that she would have liked to read about the experiences of students similar to her, before beginning the course. As a result, Mary consented to answer questions about the various aspects of being a student counsellor.

What made you decide to study counselling and psychotherapy in the first place?
 I was widowed at a very young age, which left me to bring up my children alone. When he was a young child, my eldest son experienced some behavioural issues and I was advised to see a counsellor. This seemed the best decision to make as I have always felt that talking is good, particularly where children are concerned. I always try to really listen to my kids and make them feel heard but in that instance I felt that I lacked the necessary skills. I was very impressed with the positive effect counselling had on my son and me. It was

relieving for me to be able to speak to someone about my predicament as a single mother; at the time I felt very much alone and couldn't confide in my mother or siblings, without fear of judgement. Counselling really helped.

Later, I enrolled in an adult education course entitled "An Introduction to Psychology", which really whetted my appetite. I have always been fascinated by people; their behaviour and what might be going on inside their heads. Whenever I spotted someone who appeared sad or irritated, I would wonder what set of scenarios got them to that point. As my children grew older I felt that I had acquired all this knowledge and experience which was going to waste. I frequently thought about all those children out there who needed help; help I could give them. I thought about that time when my eldest son was having difficulties in school. If he didn't have me to fight for him at that time, he might have been unfairly expelled and who knows what turn his life might have taken. He is now a balanced, successful person with his own family, but things might have been different. I felt that if I could just reach out and help other children in need, I might be able to prevent them taking the wrong road in life. It was a frustration I felt; I had the life experiences of rearing children and all that entailed but no real qualification that would enable me to work with children or young people, this thought was always in the back of my mind: "I want to get a qualification in the area of counselling."

I considered going back to college, but the thought scared me. I had left school early (third year of secondary school; intermediate certificate) and never received my leaving certificate. This fact left me lacking in confidence in relation to anything academic. I felt I just wouldn't be able for it.

Four years ago, I saw an ad in my home town, advertising a foundation course in counselling and psychotherapy. I decided to bite the bullet and enrol. The course lasted one year and I ended up with a first class honour, which went a long way to diminishing my fear of all things academic. This foundation course was absolutely crucial, particularly for someone of my age and I would recommend it to anyone in a similar position. It's an absolute must, especially if you've never been to college before.

Did you enjoy personal development?

This part of the course was bitter sweet for me. It was good to talk and have people listen to me, particularly as time progressed and I began to trust my classmates more and more. However, I found practicing in dyads and triads very difficult at first. I was reared to believe that you don't speak about your problems, you sort them out by yourself; to do so would have been seen as complaining and unnecessarily burdening someone else. To give you an example, I never heard the word "depressed" until I was married. It was ingrained in me that I should "count my blessings" and not complain. Even after my son and mother died, I still felt as though I shouldn't bother other people about my problems. It's funny, because I have no difficulty listening to the problems of others; in fact I feel that it is a privilege to be able to listen to people's stories. I am getting better at talking about my own issues and I'm slowly trying to eradicate the idea that speaking is complaining. These days, when somebody asks me how I am, I really tell them! My poor husband has to listen to a litany of issues every time he asks me how I am! Among other things, the class also really helped with this issue.

I'd also like to say a quick word about negative comments by tutors and how I dealt with it as part of my personal development. Negative comments, whether meant to hurt or not, have a real impact on me. It probably comes from my lack of confidence in my academic abilities. I really questioned whether I should continue my studies, but my drive to become a counsellor helped me through, in spite of these negative comments. I've learned a lot since starting the course, particularly in relation to those who hurt me. I have realised that I can't control what other people do or say. However, I can choose how I respond to them or their actions and that's what I try to do these days; I don't always succeed but I'm getting better at it.

How did you deal with assignments?

I received a first class honour at the end of my foundation course on counselling and psychotherapy. I remember being full of beans and relatively confident in myself at the time, but for some reason all this con diffidence drained out of me once I started the degree program. I was terrified before my first presentation; literally shaking at the knees. I thought I really messed it up but my class mates paid me a lot of nice compliments, which did help with my confidence slowly but surely. At this stage I am much more confident about public speaking. For instance, I had to make a speech at my son's wedding recently, the prospect of which would have terrified me before. I really enjoyed it and viewed the speech as my gift to him.

I like writing in general but essays are very different. I've had many sleepless nights worrying about what I would write. Every time I picked up the pen my hand would shake. I also practiced procrastination where I would choose to do anything except write my essay. Behind this anxiety was a genuine fear of being judged by the tutor. I was a bit naive at first and would write on my own terms (when I eventually mustered up the energy to write). I soon learned that if I wanted to get a good grade I had to write essays on the tutor's terms. This is very important and I would urge every student to find out exactly what the tutor wants in terms of style and content. Don't be afraid to ask them. Some like things presented in a specific way and will grade you down if you don't comply with them. Play the game by their rules and you won't go wrong.

Essays on counselling usually require a mixture of theory and personal experience. I found theory much easier to write because it's all about facts; I can go to a reference book and look everything up. It's different with personal experience.

Did you like Psychodynamic theory?

It was great to learn about Freud. He was a typical man from the Victorian era but if you accept the customs of the time and listen to his words, you'll really find a lot of interesting stuff there. Some of his theories were clearly wrong. For example, my kids (sons and daughters) didn't have a male role model growing up. They lost their father, their granddad, and their uncle around all the same time. If you were to believe Freud, my kids should be disturbed and they're not. They are all well adjusted successful adults. These theories are worth reading but they don't apply to all cases. On the other hand, I think some of Freud's theories did apply to me. I had a very strong mother and a slightly weaker father. As a kid I used to tell my friends that the opposite was true because I wished that it was. I wanted my father to be strong and lay down the law.

Humanistic psychotherapy

Rogers is my absolute favourite and Person-centred therapy is at the core of the counselling I provide, but this might change in the future. I love Roger's quietness and the way he listens to clients. People need to be listened to; they need to have their stories heard. I have one particular client who has come for 15 sessions and she is still telling her story. That's why I don't believe brief therapy (6 sessions or less) can really work. Most clients are just getting started after six sessions.

Cognitive Behaviour Therapy

CBT was the first type of psychotherapy that I was exposed to when I attended that introductory course years ago. It taught me to focus on the present; I really like its practicality and I'm looking forward to learning more about it in the future. I feel that I wasn't relaxed enough to completely absorb CBT the first time around. It was the second module in our first year of the degree program.

Have you ever tried meditation/mindfulness with clients?

I have spoken with clients about meditation/mindfulness but I haven't actually worked through a meditation with them. I have suggested how they might sit comfortably in a chair, owning their space, being aware of their breathing etc. I hope in the future, when I am more experienced, to work through meditation/breathing exercises with a client, as I have found it beneficial myself.

Is self-care important as a trainee counsellor?

I try to have quiet time, a walk or a drive by myself where I can clear my mind; I am practising meditation but not any way near to perfecting the art as yet. I find talking with my supervisor a release that helps ground me. A good way of switching off for me is to play music loudly in the kitchen and bake. I feel rejuvenated after I have met up with friends and have a good laugh; laughing is wonderful. After a day with clients I look forward to watching a soap opera or a comedy on television.

Was getting a placement difficult?

I would advise every student to think about this early on as it can be difficult to find a placement. My college was no help to me really, it was a matter of getting in touch with centres myself, sending in c.v.'s, phoning and calling in personally to various centres.

How did you feel the first time you saw a client?

I felt really nervous, like I was going into an exam. No matter how hard I tried to relax I just couldn't. I made the mistake of thinking forward; what questions would I ask? Once the session started I relaxed into it and the hour flew by. I knew then that counselling was something I really wanted to do.

Do you feel comfortable seeing clients now?

I do feel more comfortable seeing clients now. Sometimes there will be a moment of anguish or worry when the session gets 'stuck' but I access thoughts from my training and move on.

What's the best and worst thing about it?

I always look forward to meeting a client for the first time, getting to know their story. I feel privileged that this person is sharing with me, trusting me with something that maybe has never been discussed or spoken about with another person. I sometimes feel like I have been handed a very delicate and beautiful piece of art that I must be very gently with. In the beginning, if a client didn't return after a first or second session, I tended to take it personally; I felt as though I wasn't good enough to do the job. I now understand that it's not about me, it's all about the client, where they are in their life and how ready they are to tell their story. I suppose the worst thing is when a client doesn't turn up for a session, it can be frustrating. I also find it upsetting when I can't help practically, when I can see that a lot of the clients worry is financial, for instance; I know in our training we are told we are not responsible for our client but sometimes it is difficult.

What to your family and friends think about you being a counsellor?

My family and friends are all very supportive. They don't all understand why I would want to train as a counsellor. They see it as a depressive area of work but encourage me anyway. My family tell me they are proud of me and admire the dedication I have put into my training.

What is your favourite book on counselling and psychotherapy?

I haven't got a 'Bible' yet but I liked the writing of Carl Rogers, Irvin Yalom, Gerard Egan and Gerald Corry. I also love Kahil Gibran's 'The Prophet'

What advice would you give someone who wants to become a counsellor?

I would advise to give it serious thought; to become a counsellor takes a huge commitment. I would advise anyone thinking of undertaking this training to be very aware of all the costs involved. Apart from the college fees, personal counselling is mandatory and expensive. There are also supervision and clinical placement costs to be taken into account. Although it is called a part-time course, it is a huge time commitment; be aware of the amount of assignments required throughout the course; don't underestimate the amount of time sourcing information, reading books and journals and putting essays together.

There are a copious amount of notes and class hand-outs for each module during the training; I would advise to spend time reading these notes and getting into the habit of studying from the get-go. Assignment due dates come around very quickly so don't leave the reading until the last minute. Clinical placement is a big part of the training and I would advise to give this some thought from the beginning; it is not always easy to get a placement so make enquiries at an early stage.

Training to become a counsellor was a wonderful and worthwhile experience. It can be a rollercoaster of emotions. If you have considered all the difficulties and still feel this training is for you then embrace it and you will be rewarded.

Epilogue

I hope I have provided you with a convincing window into what counselling is and what it might be like to study. I have really enjoyed writing this book and learned so much more about counselling as a result. I believe that counsellors are born and not made. Yes, you can hone your communication skills, learn all about the various theories and even enhance your capacity for empathy but if you don't have that inherent hunger to really listen to suffering people you probably shouldn't be a counsellor. Extensive life experience isn't a requirement but I think it helps. Remember that suffering is part of the human experience, regardless of your position in life. If you can face your own suffering that is so often intertwined with your shadow, you will not only be the better for it, you will be a better counsellor. Try to resist the urge to fix your client. Listen and recognise what a privilege it is to hear someone else's story. And finally, lean on your class mates and fellow students, they can be your greatest support. I hope you enjoy studying counselling and psychotherapy as much as I did.

Pádraic J. Dunne

1st July 2013

Printed in Great Britain
by Amazon